D0468979

LEADERSHIP
AS AN
IDENTITY

THE FOUR TRAITS OF
THOSE WHO WIELD LASTING INFLUENCE

LEADERSHIP
AS AN
IDENTITY

CRAWFORD LORITTS

MOODY PUBLISHERS
CHICAGO

All Scripture quotations, unless otherwise indicated, are taken from *The Holy Bible, English Standard Version.* Copyright © 2000, 2001 by Crossway Bibles, a division of Good News Publishers. Used by permission. All rights reserved.

All emphases added in Scripture quotations have been placed by the author.

Editor: Dave Boehi
Interior Design: Ragont Design
Cover Design: Studio Gearbox
Cover Images: African-American man: ISP0107057, Veer
     man, hands folded: SS39087, Mel Curtis
     hands cupped: 56724490, Getty
     shoes/walking: PDP0306607, Veer

Library of Congress Cataloging-in-Publication Data

Loritts, Crawford W.
  Leadership as an identity : the four traits of those who wield lasting influence / Crawford Loritts.
  p. cm.
  ISBN 978-0-8024-5527-7
  1. Leadership—Biblical teaching. 2. Leadership—Religious aspects—Christianity. 3. Christian leadership. I. Title.
  BS680.L4L67 2009
  253—dc22

                                    2008038243

We hope you enjoy this book from Moody Publishers. Our goal is to provide high-quality, thought-provoking books and products that connect truth to your real needs and challenges. For more information on other books and products written and produced from a biblical perspective, go to www.moodypublishers.com or write to:

Moody Publishers
820 N. LaSalle Boulevard
Chicago, IL 60610

1 3 5 7 9 10 8 6 4 2

Printed in the United States of America

To Bryan, Bryndan, and Rick
Acts 20:24

CONTENTS

ANOTHER BOOK
ON LEADERSHIP?

For more than ten years now, I have had the privilege and opportunity to teach a course at Trinity Evangelical Divinity School on "The Essence of Biblical Leadership." I've also spoken on this subject at various conferences and have used the material as the foundation to mentor and encourage younger leaders. Through the years my students, colleagues, and others have encouraged me to put the content of the course in book form. For many reasons I didn't think that the time was right to do it, and besides, what more could I add to what had already been written on the topic? Certainly there is no shortage of fine books on Christian leadership already in print.

But each time I teach this material, God seems to use it to touch and change lives. I can't tell you how encouraging and gratifying it is to hear people say that these perspectives on leadership have helped them to persevere. These principles have served as the foundation for their approach to the assignments God has placed before them, gave them the courage to do the hard but right thing, and helped them to stay focused on what really matters.

Then Moody Publishers asked me what was on my heart, and I told them frankly that I was a bit conflicted. I acknowledged that I wanted to write about leadership, but I just didn't know if the project would prove to be a waste of time. After I outlined the nature and content of the book, they said that I should write it. So I am compelled to write.

Over the years I've been encouraged by many good books that have been written about leadership from a Christian perspective. Many have breathed fresh wind into my sails, stimulated my thinking, and given me help and valuable insights at important, strategic points along my journey. Authors like Ted Ingstrom, Henry Blackaby, John Maxwell, Bill Hybels, George Barna, and Hans Finzel (just to name a few) have mentored me through their writing.

Throughout the book, you'll read valuable insights on various aspects of Christian leadership from people in various roles—authors, speakers, teachers, businesspeople, administrators, educators.

Perhaps one reason these authors and so many others continue to write on leadership is because absolutely nothing of lasting value or significance will ever happen in life apart from leadership. Nothing is sustained or passed on from one generation to the next apart from leadership. God's cause and purposes in human history is advanced through faithful, focused leadership.

This is not a book about organizational structure, nor is it a "how-to" guide to leadership tasks and strategies. I won't discuss the abilities, talents, and personality traits most conducive for leadership. Instead, I will focus on something more fundamental: I want to talk about the person whom God trusts with leadership—*the person He trusts to implement and fulfill His assignments.*

Christian leadership always lives at the intersection of God, assignment, and a person.

SEARCHING THE SCRIPTURES

When I first began teaching my course on leadership there at Trinity Evangelical Divinity School, I read almost everything I could get my hands on related to leadership from a Christian perspective. Most of what I read in varying degrees proved to be very helpful. But I was left with a simple but nagging question: What does every person whom God trusts with leadership and with His assignments have in common? What do they look like? Is there a common thread?

I searched the Scriptures looking for an answer. As much as possible I tried to push aside any assumptions about what I considered to be the biblical nature of what that person looks like whom God trusts to advance His cause and His purposes. I also tried to resist the temptation to standardize or typecast the way God used some of my favorite leaders in the Bible.

What I discovered was enormously refreshing—simple and, at the same time, quite profound. For example, it almost seems as if God has a sense of humor about the kind of person to whom He chooses to entrust His assignments. Leaders in the Bible do not share common credentials—I saw an incredible diversity in educational experience, family background, and position in society. There is no particular personality type that God singles out for leadership; the personalities God uses are all over the map. The amazing stories of a sovereign God calling people from incredibly divergent backgrounds and giving them His assignments for their moment in history make it clear that He can use absolutely *anyone*.

And yet I did find some things that they had in common. I was drawn to four consistent characteristics that marked their lives and especially their leadership. I will be the first to admit that these qualities should be true of every follower of Jesus Christ, but they are especially true of every man or woman whom the Lord has called to lead. In short, distinctively Christian leaders live from and lead with these characteristics, which comprise the four sections of this book:

• Brokenness
• Uncommon communion
• Servanthood
• Radical, immediate obedience

I'm writing this book to "Christian leaders" knowing that this term encompasses a wide variety of readers. If you are a seminary student, my prayer is that this book will help you learn the initial framework of ministry and help prevent you from repeating the mistakes of more seasoned leaders. If you are a pastor or a leader in a Christian organization, I pray that these words will give you a North Star in the midst of a dizzying schedule—that it will provide perspective about God's priorities for your life. You may be working for a secular company, you may be a teacher or professor, you may be an athletic coach . . . no matter what leadership role you fill, God has raised you up for something. This book can help you discover what that is.

It is my prayer that our great God will stimulate your thinking and encourage and bless your heart as you journey through these pages. I also pray that your heart will be filled with courage and faith as you pursue God while faithfully implementing the assignments He has placed before you. Leadership is all about following His leading and experiencing Him in the process. May He be honored and glorified through our leadership!

Crawford Loritts
Atlanta, Georgia
2008

SPECIAL THANKS

In a very real sense virtually every book is a team effort. This book is no exception. I am profoundly grateful for the people who have come alongside of me to help me put on paper what has been "marinading" in my heart and mind for the past few years . . .

I am thankful for my students at Trinity Evangelical Divinity School who sat in class and interacted with me and in a very real sense helped to give shape to this book.

I am indebted to the team at Moody Publishers whose patience and encouragement kept me moving. I especially want to thank Greg Thornton, Dave DeWit, and Pam Pugh for their friendship and commitment to giving "voice" to my thoughts on leadership. I couldn't ask for a better team.

Dave Boehi is not just a friend but a wonderful partner in ministry. Dave has been invaluable in helping to give shape to what I have written. I have had the joy and privilege of working with Dave on several other writing projects and I am always impressed by his ability to capture the heart of what I am saying.

Tawnda Holley is my Executive Assistant. She is a wonderful gatekeeper, helping me to manage the activities and challenges of the clock and the calendar. Without her help I would not have gotten very far at all in putting this book together.

The Elders and the Leadership Team here at Fellowship Bible Church have given me the platform to live out what I have written about in this book. Their love for me and desire to see the Lord use what He has assigned all of us to do is a source of encouragement to me. They have given me the opportunity to demonstrate in "real time" the principles and convictions I have written about. I am grateful for their patience and grace.

Then there is Karen . . . Always Karen! We have been married now for almost thirty-eight years. She has been with me every step of the journey. Together we have experienced seasons of brokenness, uncommon communion with the Lord and with each other, learning what it means to serve, and by His grace pursuing obedience to His call and assignments for our lives. It's hard for me to imagine my life and the journey without Karen. She is the love and the joy of my life. I thank God every day for my bride!

I have been privileged to know many exceptional men and women who demonstrate faithful and outstanding lives of Christian leadership in many capacities. My thanks to the following for their contributions throughout this book:

Randy Alcorn—author and speaker
Sheila Bailey—conference speaker; president,
    E. K. Bailey Ministries
Ken Behr—former president of Evangelical Council for
    Financial Accountability

Bill Bright—The late Bill Bright was the founder and president of Campus Crusade for Christ.

Ric Cannada—chancellor of Reformed Theological Seminary

Don Carson—theologian, author

Samuel Chand—leadership consultant and author

Clyde Cook—The late Clyde Cook was a former president of Biola University.

Steve Douglass—president of Campus Crusade for Christ

Hans Finzel—president of WorldVenture; author of *Change Is Like a Slinky*

Bruce Fong—president, Michigan Theological Seminary

Bob Gerndt—retired businessman, church elder

Tim Kimmel—author and speaker

Robert Lewis—former pastor and president of LifeReady

Michael Little—president of Christian Broadcasting Network

Karen Loritts—marriage and family conference speaker (and greatest wife in the world!)

Bill McCartney—founder of Promise Keepers and currently founder and chairman of the board of the Road to Jerusalem

Dwight McKissick—pastor

Robertson McQuilken—former president of Columbia International University

George Murray—chancellor of Columbia International University

Jim Reese—successful businessman and chairman of the elders at Fellowship Bible Church

Gary Rosberg—and his wife, Barbara, are nationally known speakers; cohosts of *Dr. Gary and Barb Rosberg—Your Marriage Coaches*

Marvin Schuster—business leader

Joseph Stowell—president, Cornerstone University

Monty Watson—a teaching pastor at Fellowship Bible Church in Roswell, Georgia

Dolphus Weary—author, president of Mission Mississippi

"Whoever does the will of God abides forever."
✳ 1 JOHN 2:17

"An authentic Christian leader is spiritual. His character represents the qualities of Christ."
✳ BRUCE FONG

CHAPTER ONE

ON ASSIGNMENT
FROM GOD

All of us have at one time or another been embarrassed because we've made a wrong assumption. For example, when Bryndan, our youngest son, was a teenager,
I disciplined him for something that I just knew he had
done. In fact I was so sure that he had done it that I
wouldn't even allow him to give me an explanation.
Based on the circumstances and his past behavior, I
couldn't possibly be wrong, and I wasn't about to let him
off the hook. So I lowered the boom! I put him on re-
striction and told him that I hope he learned his lesson.

But as it turned out, I was the one who needed to
learn a lesson. Our oldest daughter came to me and
explained what really happened and let me know that
he didn't do what I thought he did. I was embarrassed,
and I had to apologize to my son.

As I look back on this experience, it's obvious that I made a wrong assumption based on the wrong information. I didn't have a clear picture of what was going on—I had the wrong perspective. I disciplined my son because I *thought* I saw behavior that was consistent with what I had seen in the past. If I had let him give me his explanation and then checked it out, I would have seen it in a different light.

I needed to get a different perspective in order to come to an accurate assessment, a right conclusion.

In the same way, we need the right perspective as we approach the subject of leadership. This sounds so simple, and the influence of our culture is so pervasive that few of us take the time to question just how modern ways of thinking cloud our minds and warp our view of true biblical leadership.

For example, as a young man I had the privilege of meeting a Christian leader whom I greatly admired. I enjoyed spending time with him, but the more I listened to him, the more concerned I became. At one point he said, "When people begin to recognize you and you get to where I am at, there's a lot of leverage in the authority I have."

It rattled me—here was a man whom God had used over the years to lead people into His kingdom, and now it seemed like he was more concerned with exerting his power and influence than he was about following God's priorities. There was a hollow ring to his words—his ministry was focused too much on him. After I left him I prayed, "God, don't let me be like him."

KEY PERSPECTIVES ON LEADERSHIP

As I have watched, read, studied, interacted with leaders, and experienced leadership through more than thirty-five years of ministry, I have come to embrace a few guiding, fundamental perspectives concerning distinctively Christian leadership. These perspectives in my mind represent a starting point that will be very helpful in our approach to leadership. There are five of them.

First, *we must fight the encroaching secularization both of Christianity in general and Christian leadership in particular.* As leaders we ought to be students of our culture, but we need to be discerning. We must learn to recognize worldviews and approaches that are human-centered rather than God-centered. Yes, by all means passionately search for principles and approaches that will help us advance His cause, but in the process let's make sure that we edit our findings through the grid of the Word of God.

The word "secular" comes from the Latin, meaning nonsacred. To be secular means that you don't believe God is foundational—He is not at the center. It doesn't necessarily mean that you are an atheist or agnostic. It just means that God is pushed out to the edges of consideration, and day-to-day operations are done from priorities and philosophies that reflect a human-centered agenda rather than a God-centered one.

We live in a Western culture that worships materialism and achievement. In our businesses and even in our churches, we think something is wrong if we aren't meeting our quarterly or yearly growth projections. We measure success by how much money we bring in or by how many people fill our worship services and Sunday school classes. This man-centered philosophy cannot help but influence our view of leadership. We look for leaders who can achieve the type of growth we expect, but we don't consider whether or not that growth reflects God's priorities.

There is a powerful, almost irresistible undertow that comes with worldly success. Over the years I've observed an unsettling pattern among many leaders who develop a track record as a "winner." When they hear people applaud them and tell them how wonderful they are . . . when high-profile people take and return their calls . . . when they begin believing they are something special . . . the success puffs them up and makes them into something different and unpleasant.

As leaders we want to get things done; we want results. And we should! This gives us a bent toward the pragmatic. However, we need to make sure that the truths and approaches we import and adopt are not contaminated. They should be consistent with what the Scriptures teach. The Word of God should be the rule, the standard for *everything* we are and do. What we believe, how we think, and how we act should be governed by our biblical framework.

Second, as a result of adopting human-centered values, *we've made too much of leadership.* I can hear you saying, "Then why are you writing this book?" and "Didn't you just say in the introduction that nothing of lasting value ever happens without leadership?"

Remember that my purpose for this book is to call us back to what the Bible emphasizes as core to true Christian leadership. And though leadership is crucial, it was never meant to be a status symbol or a personal statement of worth and value. The one who leads is no more important than the person who faithfully serves in obscurity. We have all been created in the image of God and given work to do. It is not the position that adds value to us as people—we were created with value and worth.

In our culture we have pumped up the idea of position so much that we risk sending a message that a person hasn't maximized his life unless he is moving up the corporate ladder or is recognized as a leader in our church or community. Upwardly mobile parents brag that they are raising their children to be leaders, and they send these children to schools that boast they are "building leaders for tomorrow."

We need to stop making idols out of leaders and stop idolizing the position of leadership. We need to turn down the volume and put leadership in context. As followers of Christ, we should not parrot a culture that celebrates image, stature, and position, nor should we tout leadership as the pathway to recognition and fame.

A LEADER'S WALK WITH GOD

Third, *we must avoid preferring competence over character.* Often a leader is appointed because of "what he brings to the table"—his skills and experience, his eloquence, his forcefulness and determination, his vision, his charisma, his ability to get results. But what about his walk with God? What about his family life? What about his character?

We tend to ignore character flaws and even sin in the life of a leader because of his more worldly leadership skills. Do we really want to risk all that he's doing for us by confronting him about sin? So for the sake of results and "competence," we give the leader a pass, rationalize and put a favorable spin on the issues or situation, and for the time being we declare, "life is good."

But maybe life is not good. Sooner or later problems will be apparent in both the leader and the people who are affected by his leadership. Simply stated, God never ignores or excuses sin. It's good to be good at what you do and it's a blessing to be admired and respected. But the growing competence and admiration are no substitute for the consistent nurture of your soul and the commitment to overcoming sin and pursuing Christlikeness as the focused theme of our lives.

Fourth, *we ultimately live and therefore lead before an audience of one.* Our motivation should be the glory of God. We should love Him more than anything, and all we do should be an expression of that love relationship. This includes how we lead and should be our motivation for leading. It is what John meant when he said in 1 John 2:15–17: "Do not love the world or the things in the world. If anyone loves the world, the love of the Father is not in him. For all that is in the world—the desires of the flesh and the desires of the eyes and pride in possessions—is not from the Father but is from the world. And the world is passing away along with its desires, but whoever does the will of God abides forever." The love of the Father and not the love of the world (the secular) must be our focus.

My heart is grieved and broken over the number of Christian leaders who have been seduced by "lights and the stage." When we start sharing the stage with God, eventually He lets us know—usually in a very memorable way—that He doesn't do variety shows and He's not into cohosting what He wants done in human history.

When we as leaders downplay the prominence of our walk and relationship with God, and underemphasize godly character, the Word of God, and prayer in relationship to His call for our lives, we shouldn't be surprised when we get leaders whose résumés are crammed with accomplishments but who have impoverished souls.

Fifth, *distinctive Christian leadership must be defined by the assignments given to us by God.* Recently I saw a definition of leadership that does a good job of summarizing the world's view: "Leadership is the art of getting other people to do what you want." But by its very nature, Christian leadership is different.

God's view of success is very different from that of the world. The world looks at numbers, at growth, at influence and power. But God looks at the human heart and is in the business of drawing people to Him. God gives us assignments and gives us the responsibility of leading others to implement that work. To be a leader is a sacred trust.

And here's the key: God's priorities are so different, so supernatural, that only He can fulfill them . . . and He works predominantly through leaders who remember that truth.

THE NATURE OF GOD'S ASSIGNMENTS

I believe God will make His will known to the believer who follows Him, and He will use that believer to accomplish some amazing things. What we easily forget is that these assignments are impossible for us to fulfill in our own power, because they are spiritual in nature.

Look at the final words of Christ before He ascended to heaven. Matthew 28:19–20 records that He told the disciples, "Go therefore and make disciples of all the nations, baptizing them in the name of the Father and the Son and the Holy Spirit, teaching them to observe all that I commanded you; and behold, I am with you always, even to the end of the age."

This directive is rightly called the Great Commission, and it's pretty intimidating if you think about it. Look, for example, at the phrases "make disciples of all the nations" and "teaching them to observe all that I commanded you."

Have you ever considered that you don't have the power to make even one disciple, let alone disciples in all the nations?

Have you considered that you can teach someone all the Scripture, help him grow in his faith, and model what it's like to walk with Christ, but you don't have the ability to make that person follow God?

Only God has the power to change lives. And that's why it is comforting that Jesus ended His commission with the words, "and behold, I am with you always, even to the end of the age."

The real irony is that *God's assignments involve changing your life as a leader* just as much as they involve changing the people you want to reach. God is constantly at work in building your character—making you more like Christ. He wants to build your faith as He works through you and as you encounter Him. I thought it interesting to note that Robert Lewis, a friend and former pastor, told me, "It was in leading that I encountered God the most. I saw in powerful ways His power to change lives, open doors, fulfill His promises."

Another distinctive feature of God's assignments is that they *ultimately bring Him the glory.* Leaders should not be obsessed with or defined by the *position* they occupy but by the *assignment* they have been given and the contribution they are making. Accolades may come, but the motivation for accomplishment is rooted in self-sacrifice and the faithful execution of the mission. If this brings recognition, then leaders should be humbly grateful for it, give the glory to God, and leverage the increased stature to do even more.

It's easy to lose your way in Christian leadership. If you lose sight of God's priorities, His assignments, then you lose sight of what type of leader is needed to fulfill those assignments.

But when you are attuned to God's direction and committed to fulfilling His assignments, you're on the right track. "It cannot be done without Him," says Gary Rosberg, who works with his wife, Barbara, in a ministry to strengthen marriages. "Barb and I are in so far over our heads that to bring a smidgeon of self would scare the snot out of me. If He doesn't lead, I am not going. When He does lead, I can't resist going. When we see Him glorified in what we are doing, we know we are on the road."

Godly leaders are passionate about effecting change. But they understand that the way to produce lasting impact is by *staying the same.* I'm talking about the *same* spiritual passion, fervor, and commitment to the lordship of Christ—the *same* commitment to keep the spiritual disciplines the priority and core of all that we are and all that we do. The same commitment to talk and live by the timeless, eternal values and truths from the Word of God that have transformed our lives.

In other words: The same commitment to fulfilling God's assignments.

Notes on Leadership

What are the qualities of an authentic Christian leader?

Michael Little

"Humility; inner strength (from God's Spirit); compassion; knowledge of the required topic versus faking it."

Karen Loritts

"Humility; a servant's heart; confident in God's assignment; a good listener, patient; wisdom used in communication; good reputation among peers, even critics; biblically literate; culturally aware."

Bob Gerndt

"Abiding in and depending on God; under the authority of God; humility; compassion; love for God's Word; vision; burden for the lost and for the flock; the gift of leadership."

Robert Lewis

"Knowing who I am and who I'm not (the latter is maybe even more important than the former . . . you need to build off your weaknesses and not your strengths); availability and a sensitivity to the Holy Spirit; a win-win spirit (you most enjoy others winning, not yourself); good marriage; accountable."

Bruce Fong

"Humility . . . authoritative . . . confident of God's will through knowledge of the Scripture and [they] represent truth with their life closely reflecting Christ. A Christian leader is sacrificial. They will do whatever it takes to achieve, inspire, and direct others to accomplish what God is directing to be done."

Bill McCartney

"A leader has a call of God on his life to lead. He surrounds himself with yielded, Spirit-filled staff and he serves them."

George Murray

"A close daily walk with God; spending time in His Word and in prayer; having a godly, supportive spouse; leading by influence and example, not just by position or title; decisiveness; humility; willingness to sacrifice personal prominence for the sake of the whole."

Hans Finzel

"Humility; transparency; flexibility; lifelong learning; a family and marriage that are of good reputation."

Jim Reese

"Must be a servant—willing to serve, do what you would ask others and demonstrate it not just talk it; a person of character—live your life in a way honoring to God, where you can be trusted."

Ken Behr

"A humble spirit; a heart for people; a hunger for the Word of God."

Joe Stowell

"Living a life that is worthy of respect, by living as an exemplary leader in five areas: words, conduct (particularly my conduct in regard to women, work, and wealth), love, faith, and purity!"

Dwight McKissick

"Calling, character, competence, and capacity."

Ric Cannada

"Humble; determined; godly; listens well to those around him; willing to make and stand by hard decisions; gracious; winsome."

Tim Kimmel

"• A humble heart—a reverence for God and a respect for others.

• A grateful heart—an appreciation for what he has been given and who has given it.

• A generous heart—a great delight in sharing with others what God has entrusted to him.

• A servant's heart—a willingness to take action in order to help bring the best out of everyone around him."

BROKENNESS

"Whoever abides in me and I in him, he it is that bears much fruit, for apart from me you can do nothing."

✳ JOHN 15:5

"Trust in yourself and you are doomed to disappointment; but trust in God, and you are never to be confounded in time or eternity."

✳ D. L. MOODY

CHAPTER TWO

A DESPERATE
NEED FOR GOD

Jason hung up his phone and leaned back in his padded leather chair. He felt like the world was closing in around him, and he didn't know what to do.

He looked around his office, his sanctuary—the bookcases, the framed diplomas, photos, and civic awards, the prized "I love Daddy" cards from his young children. *This is not supposed to happen to me,* he thought. *This wasn't in the plan.*

How could Emily want a divorce?

He gazed through his windows at a sky that had been washed clean by an early-morning spring storm. It was a soft, warm, sunny day. Perfect for golf. *I can hardly think. Why am I stuck in this office?*

He tried to focus on the next morning's meeting of the church elders. Three of the elders were strongly opposed to his plan to sell the church's current property and build a new campus on the outskirts of town. And now he was hearing about others in the congregation who were questioning the move.

They're stirring up dissension, he thought. *They're not submitting to authority.*

Perhaps that was Emily's problem. She needed to submit to his authority as her husband.

He wasn't accustomed to a setback like this. One of his favorite phrases in staff meetings was "Failure is not an option." That had certainly characterized his life up to this point.

He never sought to be a leader when he was younger, but it seemed as if people expected leadership from him. In the church youth group . . . in his fraternity . . . on his golf team . . . in the marketing firm where he worked for three years after college . . . people looked to him to provide fresh ideas and thorough planning. He was a clear thinker and he was eloquent—he rarely lost a debate or argument. He learned he could convince people he was right even when he knew he was wrong.

Success seemed to follow him. When he started a Bible study in his fraternity, it soon grew to over forty guys who came each week. His abilities caught the attention of the directors of the marketing firm, and he was given managerial responsibilities within a year. When he shocked everyone and announced he was resigning his job to follow God's call to attend seminary, his boss called up the seminary president just to let him know what kind of young man he was getting.

And now here he was, the thirty-two-year-old pastor of a church that had grown by more than five hundred people since he took over. The local newspaper had recently run a large article on the church, with a large photo of him preaching. *I've put this church back on its feet,* he thought. *Everybody loves my sermons.*

I'm introducing fresh ways to worship God and reach out into the community.

Now it seemed like everything was falling apart. The church leadership wasn't as unified as it had been before. He had more trouble convincing people that his decisions were correct. The church hadn't grown in a year.

He was beginning to wonder if God might be leading him somewhere else—to a church where they would appreciate his leadership. But now Emily had filed for divorce, and that might mess everything up.

He had to admit that their relationship had become contentious. He had a hard time talking with her—she just wouldn't listen to him. She was getting stubborn. "Just because you can outtalk me doesn't mean you're right," she had said.

How could Emily want a divorce when we've always said that we'd never even consider it?

What's this going to do to the kids?

What's wrong with her? How could she do this to us?

YOU CAN'T DO IT ON YOUR OWN

What do you think God is doing in Jason's life?

I admit he is a composite character—I don't know anyone in his precise situation. And yet there is much in Jason that is typical of many leaders I have known through the years. His world is crumbling; he is at a crossroads.

Put simply, Jason is a proud man who needs to be humbled. If he wants to see God work through him in the future as He has in the past, Jason needs to let go and realize he is not in control of his ministry and his family. He cannot do it on his own.

He needs to be broken.

He needs God.

Brokenness is a *conscious, core awareness that you need God in all things.* A broken person has come to realize that he is nothing and can do nothing apart from God's presence and enabling power (John 15:5). A broken person has come to the end of himself—at least what he understands at that moment to be the end of himself.

For a Christian leader, brokenness is a dear friend, and pride is the enemy. When you are broken, you realize *you cannot do it in your own power*—you cannot earn salvation on your own, you cannot walk with God on your own, and you cannot fulfill God's assignments on your own.

Why? Because of the very nature of God's assignments. As I wrote in the last chapter, God's assignments revolve around His priorities—helping people know Him and walk with Him. The very nature of what He wants done is supernatural. He uses human instruments to do what is impossible.

AN ONGOING PROCESS

The leader who is broken is a leader who can be used by God. As Isaiah 57:15 (NASB) tells us, "For thus says the high and exalted One Who lives forever, whose name is Holy, 'I dwell on a high and holy place, and also with the contrite and lowly of spirit in order to revive the spirit of the lowly and to revive the heart of the contrite.'"

Brokenness is not a onetime event. It is never finished; it's an ongoing process. In her excellent book *Brokenness: The Heart God Revives*, Nancy Leigh DeMoss writes:

> *Brokenness is not a feeling or an emotion. Rather, it requires a choice, an act of the will. Further, this choice is not primarily a onetime experience, though there may be profound and life-changing spiritual turning points in our lives. True brokenness is an ongoing, constant*

way of life. True brokenness is a lifestyle—a moment-by-moment lifestyle of agreeing with God about the true condition of my heart and life—not as everyone else thinks it is but as He knows it to be.[1]

I have been brought face-to-face with brokenness. In fact, there have been entire seasons of brokenness in my life, times in which I had no choice but to embrace my complete inadequacy.

I have felt the sting of failure. I have tasted what it feels like to be let down by friends when you needed them most. I know something of what it's like to be betrayed.

I have sampled the experience of God seemingly turning a deaf ear to my cries for His help and intervention. I have faced the rapid series of one overwhelming crisis after another, many of which left me numb and disoriented.

I know what it means to have others depend on me for leadership and yet feel fearful, overwhelmed, and alone. The very contradiction is a screaming reminder of my inadequacy. And yes, I know what it's like to have to keep ministering and leading even when the confidence has been knocked out of me.

Through all these experiences, one clear message was clear: Crawford, you desperately need God!

INADEQUACY—A POSITIVE TRAIT

Author and Christian leader Randy Alcorn says that to him brokenness "is more than just periodic times of intense emotional experience, it's an ongoing sense of inadequacy. When I come to a point, as I face life's difficulties, where I know I can't just fix things, including myself, it's a much needed reminder that He is the Vine, I am a branch, and apart from Him I can do nothing.

"Sometimes well-meaning people have tried to talk me out of this sense of inadequacy. But this sense is vital to fruitful ministry.

Furthermore, it's rooted in reality—in and of ourselves we are inadequate, and we must come to terms with that. When I don't recognize my inadequacy, I trust myself rather than Christ."

Can you imagine a more startling statement for leaders? Randy's comment that a sense of inadequacy is "vital to fruitful ministry" runs contrary to the way the world looks at leadership. Think about it: Most people are hired and achieve success because of the gifts, talents, abilities, and experiences they bring to the table. If a church is looking for a pastor, or if a company is looking for a new vice president, they search for someone with the right set of skills and experiences. How often do you hear them say, "We're looking for someone who is inadequate for the job"?

In our world, leaders are chosen because of their abilities and experience. The more success they see as a leader, the more they grow in confidence—and the more they are tempted, such as Jason in my opening story, to take pride in their gifts and abilities. This is a pitfall for young leaders and older leaders alike.

Think of the young man working in a Christian organization who is quickly recognized for his "leadership skills." He is bold and decisive, he works hard, he presents his views clearly and forcefully, and people are drawn to him. He may move quickly into a position of influence because his superiors are impressed with these skills, when in reality he may lack the spiritual grounding and maturity required of his new position.

Another common pitfall for younger leaders is the conceit of youth—the idea that tried-and-tested ideas and older colleagues are hopelessly out of touch and that new ideas are superior. Again, our culture promotes this belief. I remember the phrase that the Baby Boom generation created: "Never trust anyone over thirty." Each new generation feels that they can do things much better than the previous one did.

"Young leaders tend to be full of pride and self-sufficiency and a generational arrogance that comes with being twenty and thirty," says Hans Finzel. "This should be recognized as a danger sign!"

Ken Behr echoes these thoughts: "Pride is one of the easiest ways for a younger leader to lose their influence. Pride tells us 'we can do' while we need to understand that the wisdom that is needed is godly. Pride will also stop us from seeking others' advice and will often lead to quick, rash decisions and subpar results."

These are men who know the truth of their words—because they were once young themselves.

Likewise, an older leader can fall into a similar trap. For years he has progressed in power and influence, and he has grown confident in his abilities. His track record in making important decisions leads him to believe that his opinions are usually the correct ones. After years, and even decades, of success, he develops a sense of arrogance and infallibility.

In reality, these leaders are depending on their natural abilities, and at some point they will realize that these abilities only take them so far. In a Christian ministry, you eventually will realize there are some things only God can do.

HOW TO BE MOST USEFUL TO GOD

Clyde Cook pointed out that brokenness gave him the realization that he was weak and that he could fail. He further observed, "Too often, especially after some successes, you can rely on your own ingenuity and strength and not realize that without the Lord Jesus Christ you can do nothing."

It's good to be reminded that we are most useful to God when we realize that in ourselves we don't have what it takes to get His assignments done. The reason we are inadequate is because God wants us and everybody else to know that what has been accomplished has been done in His strength and for His glory.

There is always a gap between what you have and what God wants done. You won't always see how it can be done. And so you're faced with a choice. Either you allow the magnitude of the challenge to overwhelm you, or you surrender all your deficiencies to Him, acknowledging that the *only* way you can accomplish the assignment is if He does it through you.

As I write these words I sense my own inadequacy. As the senior pastor of a growing church, I know I am always in over my head. To care for and love the people, provide leadership in multiple areas at the same time, to study and preach week after week with a heart and mind that pursues excellence, to deal with the occasional crisis, to keep my heart and mind spiritually refreshed, and to keep Karen and our marriage a focused priority demands more than I have in me to give.

But it is this wonderful sense of helpless inadequacy that keeps me running to our loving, gracious, and, yes, merciful heavenly Father for His strength. I have learned that He loves to hear me say, "Father, I can't do what You have called me to do without You. In fact, I can't make it without You. If You don't come through, it's all over. Please, Father, do Your work through me!" And time and again I can hear Him whispering those sweet words, "Crawford, you are where I want you to be. Place all that is before you in My hands, trust Me and I will accomplish through you what I have called you to do."

God loves to be depended on. So He gives imperfect, inadequate human beings impossible assignments.

"When pride comes, then comes disgrace, but with the humble is wisdom."

＊ PROVERBS 11:2

"It is wonderful what God can do with a broken heart if He gets all the pieces."

＊ SAMUEL CHADWICK

CHAPTER THREE

SURRENDERING

TO GOD

Surrender is the leader's response to his brokenness. Surrender demonstrates that he always and forever needs God.

God delights in surrender. It is a foundational, fundamental principle of the Christian life. In fact, you can't truly be a Christian without surrender. Turning from your sin and self-reliance and putting your trust in Christ for His love and forgiveness is a profound act of surrender. And God wants you to *keep* turning from yourself and *continually* be turning over to Him all that you are and all that He has placed in your hands to work with.

It is from this place of surrender that your life is transformed and you become the expression of God's unique mission for your moment in history. Pay close attention to what the apostle Paul says in Romans 12:1–2: "I appeal to you therefore, brothers, by the mercies of God, to present your bodies as a living sacrifice, holy and acceptable to God, which is your spiritual worship. Do not be conformed to this world, but be transformed by the renewal of your mind, that by testing you may discern what is the will of God, what is good and acceptable and perfect."

Notice that your ability to discern God's will is directly related to presenting your body as a "living sacrifice." But it's also important to note that you don't surrender to Him just because you want insights on what His will is; you surrender primarily because He has been merciful. As an act of worship driven by gratitude, you give your life to Him. He then gives you the ability to know what He wants to do through your life. Your very life has been sacrificed to God to do whatever He wants to do.

LEADERS WHO STOP FOLLOWING

Effective Christian leadership is sustained by surrender. When a Christian leader stops yielding to God, he or she has ceased to be a Christian leader. It's really quite simple. When a leader gets to a point at which he or she trusts more in skills, abilities, or experiences to accomplish God's assignments, then he has just walked away from the place of God's blessing and His enabling power.

Dr. Joseph Stowell, an outstanding Christian leader, served for many years as the president of the Moody Bible Institute in Chicago. Joe is a dear friend, and recently we were ministering together at a pastors conference. As he addressed these leaders, I heard him say something that was so very simple and yet so profound. He said that "leaders fall when they stop following."

Think about that. When a leader shifts his focus from dependently following Christ and begins to think that it is *his* vision, *his* idea, and *his* mission that must be advanced, then he has ceased to be God's leader. And, frankly, it's dangerous to follow such a person. At this point there is nothing supernatural about what he does; he is merely a strong personality who can get things done by the force of his will. He may try to camouflage it with a few Bible verses and Christian clichés, but pride and self-determination are what drive him. And this, in turn, affects the organization or ministry.

This is a very common pitfall.

Power and influence can change people and not always for the good. When you are aware of your inadequacies and very few people pay attention to you, it's not so difficult to pursue a surrendered life. But the more successful you become, and the more recognition you receive from that success, the more difficult it is to embrace humility and to remember your constant need for His grace and mercy.

My heart aches even as I write these words. Flashing across my mind are friends and colleagues who stopped following; people God had used in marvelous ways until they forgot that it was God who used them. I have felt the temptation myself to forget that.

I'm thinking of a man who started out with a heart that was pure and undivided. There was a sweet humility about him and a passion to do whatever the Lord wanted him to do. And God blessed his life and ministry in tremendous ways. It was meteoric. His ministry was growing so fast that he couldn't keep up with the demands and requests for his time. He was like a magnet. People and resources were drawn to him.

But somewhere along the way something happened to him. Sadly, he hasn't handled the prominence and the visibility too well. If you had known him in the early days of his ministry, you'd almost want to say that this isn't the same person! There's an arrogance and swagger about him that's not very inviting. I am praying that he will go back to that place of sweet surrender before God deals with him.

This sort of reminds you of King Uzziah, doesn't it?

The demise of King Uzziah in my mind is one of the most tragic stories in the Bible. I am convinced that God wanted all of us, particularly Christian leaders, to see the devastating consequences when a leader allows his pride to make assumptions about God and the work He has given us to do.

The twenty-sixth chapter of 2 Chronicles describes how Uzziah was only sixteen when he became king of Judah and he reigned for more than fifty-two years (26:3). God used Uzziah greatly for most of his tenure as king for one simple reason: He sought the Lord. Look at these words in verses 4 and 5: "And he did what was right in the eyes of the Lord, according to all that his father Amaziah had done. *He set himself to seek God* in the days of Zechariah, who instructed him in the fear of God, *and as long as he sought the Lord, God made him prosper.*"

Uzziah built a powerful army and subdued his enemies. He amassed a fortune. He was respected, honored, and followed. The source of his accomplishments is given to us in this incredible line in verse 15: "And his fame spread far, for he was marvelously helped."

Who helped him? Was it his family? Was it his soldiers? How about his smarts, his strategic thinking? No, God made him what he was and gave him what he had.

And then, at the pinnacle of his success, it all fell apart.

At the pinnacle of his success, Uzziah did a tragically foolish thing. Verse 16 of chapter 26 tells us, "But when he was strong, he grew proud, to his destruction. For he was unfaithful to the

Lord his God and entered the temple of the Lord to burn incense on the altar of incense."

In God's eyes he reached the tipping point; he crossed the line. What was the problem?

A LESSON FROM UZZIAH'S PLAYBOOK

First, *Uzziah stopped seeking God when he became strong.* God wants you to always remember that you are being carried by Him each step of the way. Always yield and surrender to Him because you know how easily your flesh can deceive you. If you don't surrender your accomplishments and successes to Him as an act of worship and thanksgiving, you will foolishly conclude that what has been accomplished is all because of your abilities.

It usually is a very gradual thing. With a few successes and victories, you begin to lose the awe and wonder of God's blessing. Praise and thanksgiving slowly give way to the celebration of strategies and principles and the *person* at the center of the success. God fades from the foreground to the backdrop. You now occupy center stage, and because of a track record of success, you start making dangerous assumptions about God, leadership, and your abilities. Inevitably you cross the line, and God deals directly with you.

Second, because Uzziah stopped seeking God, *he no longer surrendered his heart as well as the successes back to God as a statement of recognition that it is always, only about Him.* His head got big and he lost perspective. Humility is an intentional thing. It is a decision, a choice. When you fail to intentionally humble yourself, pride will overtake you. It's just a matter of time. And God goes after pride *every* time, especially when it raises its ugly head in leaders (James 4:6).

Third, *in his pride Uzziah reached beyond the role and responsibility to which God had called him.* Uzziah was called to be the king, but he was not called to be a priest. He apparently thought that, since he was so eminently successful, he had the right to do almost anything he wanted to do. So he entered the temple of the Lord and burned incense on the altar. But this was the domain of the priest, and Uzziah knew better.

King Uzziah positioned himself for a hard, devastating fall. And that's exactly what happened. He allowed the lethal cocktail of consistent success and unchecked pride to push him past the point of no return. God's judgment was swift, tragic, and final.

Second Chronicles 26:16–21 tells us what happened next. Even after Azariah the priest and eighty other priests begged Uzziah to stop and warned him ("Go out of the sanctuary, for you have done wrong, and it will bring you no honor before the Lord"), he refused! He became indignant and angry. Didn't they know his track record and hadn't they witnessed his rise to prominence? What right did they have to even suggest that as a leader he was accountable for his actions? Didn't they realize that he was beyond that?

As a result, God Himself came after Uzziah. When the king resisted the priests, he broke out with leprosy (verse 19). Leprosy in the Old Testament was the epitome of what it meant to be unclean. Lepers could not be touched, and they were permanently separated from the rest of the population. People would not come near a leper.

Uzziah remained a leper for the rest of his life, "and being a leper lived in a separate house, for he was excluded from the house of the Lord" (verse 21). It's almost as though God said to him, "Because you stopped seeking and surrendering to me, now others will no longer come close to you." God took away from Uzziah what He Himself had given to him in the first place—prominence, popularity, and influence.

All of us who are leaders should be sobered and gripped by the demise of Uzziah. Don't ever forget that it's God who is working through you—your accomplishments are not a statement of your glory but of the grace, power, and glory of God Almighty.

The only way to maintain this perspective is to regularly and joyfully surrender all that you are back to Him. One of the most important ways to do this is to take the compliments people give you and give them back to God as a praise offering. When God blesses you with the fulfillment of a vision He has placed on your heart or with the accomplishment of a goal, set aside a time to celebrate and praise God for what He has done through you and for you.

Whenever possible, do this publicly. It's important that those who work closely with you or who follow your leadership *see* you giving glory to God. This is a profound act of surrender. And heartfelt, sincere praise is a powerful reminder that as leaders we are submissive followers.

Remember the words of Joe Stowell: "Leaders fall when they stop following."

How's your surrender?

Notes on Leadership

How has brokenness affected your life and enriched your approach to leadership?

Hans Finzel

"Brokenness is an essential pathway that we must travel to get to effective leadership. Pride gets in the way; humility empowers leaders. The way that pride is crushed is through brokenness that can come through hardship, tragedy, or thorns in the flesh. It has been a huge part of my preparation for leadership—to be broken and stay broken before Him."

Steve Douglass

"Times I have been broken by the Lord have helped me grow in my relationship with Him. That has helped me not unduly 'rescue' people when God is working similarly in their lives."

Dwight McKissick

"Brokenness has caused me to depend less on me and more on God. It has also given me patience toward others as I realize God has been patient with me. Leadership is often birthed out of brokenness."

Marvin Schuster

"Resulted in salvation; gave me a dose of humility; allowed me to see my shortcomings; changed my spirit of superiority to a serving spirit."

Ken Behr

"I don't think I really understood brokenness until my children and wife [started] training a number of horses. . . . a large, powerful, and muscular horse was only useful if it was broken and submissive to its master. As I've become broken and submissive to what God wants for my life and my ministry, it certainly has made me a better servant leader and more focused on the kingdom rather than my own agenda."

Jim Reese

"I believe that one of the biggest things that brokenness has contributed to me in regard to leadership is empathy and a desire to understand the other person and be sensitive to move the other person forward even when you might be having a very difficult discussion. I probably approach most discussions working to understand where the other person is. Brokenness also breaks the spirit of pride and creates even more dependence on God."

Bob Gerndt

"C. S. Lewis' statement that 'God whispers to us in our pleasures . . . and shouts to us in our pain' relates to my experience exactly. My approach to leadership is one that recognizes that intellectual learning can only take us so far . . . and not very far at that. We must ask God to turn our learning into living, and He so often uses physical, emotional, and spiritual pain to do that."

Dolphus Weary

"When my son Reggie was diagnosed with cancer in the early 80s, we were broken; when he was killed, we were broken again. It has made me realize that God wants us to keep going and doing what we can while we can."

Tim Kimmel

"God's Word says, 'Humble yourselves, therefore, under God's mighty hand that he may lift you up in due time' (1 Peter 5:6). The sooner a young Christian leader figures out that God has given him the job of humbling himself, the sooner God will be able to hand more responsibility to that leader."

Ric Cannada

"Brokenness (from events such as the death of my brother from cancer when he was nineteen and I was twenty-one, and also some of my own sins as well as the sins of my children) has humbled me as a servant leader, and made me more sensitive to the needs and hurts of others as I seek to challenge and motivate them to serve the Lord."

"For you will not delight in sacrifice, or I would give it; you will not be pleased with a burnt offering. The sacrifices of God are a broken spirit; a broken and contrite heart, O God, you will not despise."

✳ Psalm 51:16–17

"Your heart for God may be . . . destroyed by allowing the fires of jealousy, anger, self-pity, worry, or gluttony to go unchecked in your life."

✳ Nancy Leigh DeMoss

CHAPTER FOUR

FALLING INTO SIN

One of the godliest men I've ever known was Bill Bright. Bill was in many ways an unassuming man, but God gave him the incredible assignment of building a movement that would proclaim the gospel around the world. Under his leadership Campus Crusade for Christ grew to be the largest parachurch organization of its kind, as well as one of the most effective evangelistic movements in the history of the church. My wife and I had the privilege of serving with Campus Crusade for twenty-seven years, and today I serve as a member of the board of directors.

Bill was a man who seemed to walk and work in a state of continual worship. And yet he never lost his sense of how weak and fragile he was; he never forgot that he was a sinner. I recall hearing him say many times, "Please pray for me. I don't want to lose my first love. I don't want to do anything that would bring shame to my Savior."

He understood that God's blessing and favor on Campus Crusade for Christ did not mean that he was somehow less capable of falling into sin. If anything, he clearly understood that the awesome, holy God of the universe had entrusted a vision and an assignment to a mere man who had weaknesses and temptations like everyone else. And he wasn't afraid to let others know that he needed the prayers of God's people to help him to overcome and to finish well. His humility and sincerity drew your heart to him. You wanted to follow his leadership because he was aware of how much he needed God and His strength to resist the pull toward sinful disobedience.

In this regard Bill Bright was just like the rest of us. When a leader operates from a position of brokenness, he realizes that he is capable of sinful failure.

ONE DECISION AWAY

It's important to understand that as long as we are standing on this side of heaven we are very capable of hurting the heart of God, betraying His trust, and damaging the cause of Christ. As Jim Reese, a businessman and the chairman of the elders at our church, says, "A challenge not only for young leaders but for all leaders is that you are one decision away from losing the ability to lead."

Seeking God and surrendering to Him has to be a disciplined process because the struggle and battle with the flesh is never over. Tim Kimmel points out that "Brokenness empowers a leader because it forces him or her to do more than lip service to the grace of God. When we realize how utterly helpless we are and how utterly self-destructive we are capable of being when left to our own devices, we gain a better understanding of just how amazing God's grace really is."

The apostle Paul touched on this theme several times in his epistles. In 1 Timothy 3:6–7, for example, he writes that a leader "must not be a recent convert, or he may become puffed up with conceit and fall into the condemnation of the devil. Moreover, he must be well thought of by outsiders, *so that he may not fall into disgrace, into a snare of the devil.*"

Also, take a look at Paul's direct, sobering words to the young leader Timothy:

> Now in a great house there are not only vessels of gold and silver but also of wood and clay, some for honorable use, some for dishonorable. Therefore, if anyone cleanses himself from what is dishonorable, he will be a vessel for honorable use, set apart as holy, useful to the master of the house, ready for every good work. So flee youthful passions and pursue righteousness, faith, love, and peace, along with those who call on the Lord from a pure heart.
> ✳ 2 TIMOTHY 2:20–22

Finally, notice how intentional and passionate Paul is about his life and ministry as he shares his heart motivation in 1 Corinthians 9:24–27:

> Do you not know that in a race all the runners compete, but only one receives the prize? So run that you may obtain it. Every athlete exercises self-control in all things. They do it to receive a perishable wreath, but we an imperishable. So I do not run aimlessly; I do not box as one beating the air. But I discipline my body and keep it under control, *lest after preaching to others I myself should be disqualified.*

NOBLE ASSIGNMENTS

There are three big lessons in these passages.

First, *the lives we lead as leaders should be well-thought-of by a watching world.* People may not agree with us and they may even despise what we stand for, but we should never give them an objective reason to reject us and what we believe due to the sinful inconsistency of our lives. How many times have we seen Christianity ridiculed in the press over the past two decades because an outspoken leader fell into the very type of sin he publicly condemned?

Second, *our lives should match the message and the noble assignments that God entrusts to us.* This is what Paul means by being a vessel of honor. God wants to serve His meals on clean plates. Our job is to make sure that our lives are clean. Again, God is not so much concerned about our abilities and gifts as He is about our personal holiness. We have to keep the plate clean.

Third, *leaders have been and will be disqualified by God if we do not run His race according to His rules.* God does not put up with sin. And if we continue to sin, He will take His assignments away from us and declare us unusable and replace us with someone else who will live for Him (1 Samuel 15). And in some cases the failure to clean up our lives will be the cause of physical death (1 John 5:16–17).

I am not saying that godly leaders never sin. But what I am saying is that patterns of sin should not dominate our lives and our call to lead must be viewed as a call to Christlikeness in every area of our lives. Overcoming sin and keeping our hearts and lives pure is our passion. We want people to follow us because we are following Christ. We're not just telling people what Jesus said; we are by His grace and strength living what He said.

A PULL TOWARD SIN

It is true that God will use our past failures, as in the case of King David's adultery and murder (2 Samuel 11) and Peter's denial of Jesus (Matthew 26:69–75). These failures break God's heart and, if followed by repentance, keep our hearts tender, producing a sweet God-dependent life. But failure should not be the primary source of our brokenness. It is the ever-present realization that we *could* hurt His heart—that we carry within us a pull toward sin—that ought to keep us pushing toward God. We should be most afraid when we forget that we need His help to stand, "Therefore let anyone who thinks that he stands take heed lest he fall" (1 Corinthians 10:12).

In an essay entitled "Becoming a Leader of No Reputation," Scott Rodin wrote of his convictions about leadership after serving for several years as a seminary president:

> *If I could put one Bible verse on the desk of every pastor and every Christian leader in the world, it would be this, "If we say that we have no sin, we deceive ourselves and the truth is not in us" (1 John 1:8). As Christian leaders we must be engaged in a constant process of self-evaluation and repentance. It is so easy for us to be tempted in a variety of directions, and when we stray, we impact our entire ministry. Good leaders undertake their work with a deep humility and a keen awareness of their own weaknesses and shortcomings.[2]*

Again, this humility is what I observed and learned as I watched Bill Bright and so many other leaders who have and are influencing my life. Their conscious awareness that they are capable of being overcome by sin produces a humility and authenticity that draws people to them but, more important, draws the attention and favor of God to them (1 Peter 5:5–6). As leaders we should plead with God to help us to never forget this.

LIVING HIS LIFE THROUGH US

Leaders need to be particularly aware of whose life is on display. Our brokenness reminds us that *Christ must live His life through us.* Galatians 2:20 says, "I have been crucified with Christ. It is no longer I who live, but Christ who lives in me. And the life I now live in the flesh I live by faith in the Son of God, who loved me and gave himself for me."

Those who follow you as leaders should see Christ both in terms of who you are and in how you go about fulfilling the assignments God has given to you. Your human tendency for sin should drive you to the cross, shouting all the way that you need Jesus. When you place your brokenness at the foot of the cross, you declare that you have nothing to prove and that Jesus Christ Himself makes Himself known through mortal, fragile human beings.

"Cursed is the man who trusts in man and makes flesh his strength, whose heart turns away from the Lord."

✴ JEREMIAH 17:5

"When God's warrior marches forth to battle strong in his own might, defeat is not far distant."

✴ CHARLES SPURGEON

CHAPTER FIVE

THE STRENGTH
OF WEAKNESS

Weakness is despised by most leaders, he says. Weakness is the enemy.

"Strong leaders," says author and speaker Steve Farrar, "do not want to be weak."

What an irony. In reality, that pride that leads us to abhor weakness is perhaps the most deadly weakness of all.

Instead, you should welcome your weakness, even celebrate it. Weakness means that you are usable.

I am intrigued by the words of the apostle Paul, who wrote, "If I must boast, I will boast of the things that show my weakness" (2 Corinthians 11:30). I consider Paul one of the most dynamic leaders of the Bible, and it's obvious that his contemporaries viewed him the same way.

Yet in this passage he says he boasts in his weakness. He goes on to describe his struggle with what he called a "thorn in the flesh." Although Paul prayed, even with his apostolic authority, that it would be removed from him, God would not take it away. Instead Jesus told him, "My grace is sufficient for you, for my power is made perfect in weakness" (2 Corinthians 12:9).

Whatever this "thorn" was, it reminded Paul of how weak he was and how much he needed God's strength. Further, the message from Jesus is loud and clear: Our Lord is not limited by your weaknesses. Instead, His power is more complete *because* of them. When you are inescapably reminded of how desperate you are for God, it's amazing how quickly you get out of His way and allow Him to do what He wants to do through your life.

I want to encourage you to stop looking at your limitations as hindrances or anchors to God working through your life. The fact that you don't feel qualified to do what you are doing may be the very reason why God has placed you where you are. You are reminded daily that if God doesn't come through for you, you are dead in the water.

I have a friend who once was a drug dealer and served time in prison. While in prison he gave his life to Jesus Christ. He fell deeply in love with Jesus and began to grow in his faith. When he was released he was discipled by an older pastor and in the process discovered that God had given him leadership abilities. Today my friend is a leader in a well-known Christian organization and is responsible for directing hundreds of people. God is using him in great ways.

But if you would ask him what he struggles with the most, he would tell you that often his background and lack of formal education sometimes make him feel terribly inadequate. Then you would take a look at the tremendous fruit of his life and ministry and scratch your head and say, "Are you kidding me?" God's strength has been perfected in his weakness. God is using him greatly *because* of his limitations.

What about you? Weaknesses come in all shapes and sizes— broken relationships, strong temptations, depression, tragic loss, feelings of inadequacy, mistreatment. It really doesn't make any difference what it is. The question is: What do you do with your weaknesses, failures, and wounds? Do you hand them over to God in exchange for His grace and strength, or do you wallow in self-pity, allowing the enemy of your soul to immobilize you?

GOOD REASONS? OR POOR EXCUSES?

Nowhere is this tendency better illustrated than in the third chapter of Exodus, which describes how God gave Moses an unexpected and incredible assignment: to lead Israel out of bondage and slavery to the Egyptians. By this time Moses was eighty years old and apparently had grown accustomed to the life of a shepherd. Long gone was his desire to rescue his fellow Jews from the hands of the Egyptians (Exodus 2:11–15). He had zero ambition to be the leader of the Jews, much less God's man to lead their deliverance from slavery. But that is precisely what God called Moses to do. God dramatically appeared to Moses in the form of a burning bush and in no uncertain terms told Moses that he was His man for the job (Exodus 3:1–10).

Imagine how absurd this task must have appeared to Moses. How could he, an eighty-year-old exile, lead an enslaved people out of a nation as powerful as Egypt? It's a humanly impossible job, and it is obvious from the text that Moses knew it. He was overwhelmed with a sense of inadequacy and proceeded to present God with four excuses of why he was not the one for the job.

Excuse #1: "I'm a nobody now and Pharaoh won't give me the time of day" (3:11).

Excuse #2: "I have no authority or credibility with the Jews" (3:13).

Excuse #3: "The Jews won't believe me" (4:1).

Excuse #4: "I am not a good speaker" (4:10).

God answered Moses with two powerful illustrations (Exodus 4:3–9). First, He told Moses to take the staff that he had used as a shepherd and throw it on the ground. Moses obeyed and watched the stick become a snake! Then God told Moses to grab the snake by the tail. As soon as he did, the snake returned to its form as his familiar staff.

Next, God told Moses to take his eighty-year-old hand and place it inside of his cloak. As soon as he did, the hand became leprous. Once again God told Moses to take that same hand and put it back inside his cloak. When Moses obeyed, the hand was restored.

God specifically answered all of Moses' arguments by pointing to His sufficiency. It was as if God was saying, "Moses, will you take your eyes off of yourself and take a look at who is giving you this assignment? Don't worry about your authority or credibility. Don't worry about whether the Jews will believe you. Don't worry about your personal weaknesses. I will supply everything you need."

I think the lesson from these two miracles is that God does not primarily delight in using what you bring to the table. Instead, He delights in using *what you surrender to Him.* His assignments will require you to operate outside of your areas of strength, out of your comfort zone. God will put you in situations where you have no choice but to rely on His miraculous power, strength, and intervention.

The fact is that leaders are always in over their heads. That's because God's assignments are supernatural in nature and He gives those assignments to vessels of clay—cracked, chipped clay pots! His holy, noble calling is placed in the hands of fragile, weak humanity.

I have come to firmly believe that inadequacy is always associated with anything that God calls us to do. If as a leader you do not feel weak, you may very well have to answer two fundamental questions. First, have you been ambushed by pride, giving you a false sense of capacity and security? Second, are you really doing what God called you to do?

YOU CAN'T DO IT ALL

Our weaknesses should also remind us how much we need other people. One common problem with leaders is a bit of a paradox —they direct other people, yet they may hold on too fiercely to responsibilities they should delegate to others.

It's important for leaders to realize they can't do it all. They don't have the time to do it all, and they don't have the skills to do it all.

It's interesting that many leaders don't bemoan their weakness in completing administrative work. They know they couldn't survive without the help of a capable administrative assistant. Yet they run themselves into the ground trying to keep up with too many other tasks. For example, it's impossible for many pastors to keep up with all the counseling needs in their congregations, or to adequately meet the needs of all the sick, injured, or grieving individuals. And while it's important for them to be involved in meeting those needs, they also need to delegate some of those responsibilities to others.

Awareness of your weaknesses should also help make you more sympathetic to the challenges faced by other leaders who are tackling the assignments God has given them.

When I became a senior pastor a few years ago, I was deeply moved and encouraged by other pastors in our community and across the country who reached out to me. Locally, Bryant Wright, Andy Stanley, and Randy Pope met with me to offer their encouragement and support. These are veteran leaders who pastor large, influential churches ministering to thousands every week.

What impressed me most was their humility. I sensed in each of these men a care and compassion born out of a gratitude to God that they would be called and privileged to serve. They knew what I was facing and they met with me to let me know that they are with me. Not one of them spoke of how important and successful he is. I got the distinct impression that they are just grateful that God would use them. They know they are men with weaknesses.

UNHEALTHY BROKENNESS

At the same time, our weaknesses and inadequacies, whatever they may be, should not cause us to be stuck and overwhelmed by an unhealthy, wounded condition. I've talked with some people who are very open and honest about their weaknesses and distress, but I've wondered whether they've really dealt with them in a healthy way. They can't seem to resolve their hurt and pain—they are paralyzed from moving forward.

This is a tricky subject to address, because some people have been wounded deeply during their lives, and some struggle with weaknesses that are almost overpowering. I want to be sensitive to them. At the same time, I feel the struggle we face should be the opportunity to experience the liberating power and grace of God as we acknowledge how fragile and dependent we are before a holy God and we go to Him for the help that we so desperately need.

God does not want us to wear the immobilizing paralysis of our wounds and pain as a badge of brokenness. But rather He wants us to pursue healing and point to His power in the midst of our weakness. Brokenness is a statement about how *God* ministers to us and through us because we have allowed our weaknesses to drive us to His heart. Authentic brokenness always casts the spotlight on the glory of God and not the fact that we struggle.

Theologian and author Don Carson puts it in perspective when he says, "It is possible to be so broken that one's life is characterized rather more by depression and even despair than by renewed strength in leadership. In other words, brokenness does not *guarantee* enriched leadership. It is a mark of the Lord's kindness when He so providentially overrules such that the brokenness engenders humility, recognition of one's weakness and potential for failure, and renewed eagerness to trust the Lord."

Carson's words remind us that there is such a thing as an unhealthy brokenness. Unfortunately I have known more than a few Christian leaders who have spiritualized their emotional hurts and pain, passing it off as brokenness.

WHEN MISTAKES ARE MADE

Failure is part of the learning and molding process for a leader. And often this failure is the result of sin and pride. One leader wrote to me, "I could write a multivolume series on this one. I have had more egg on my face than most."

The responses to my leadership questionnaire on this subject were consistent and enlightening. They seemed to emphasize two critical points:

First, *admit your error.* Assume responsibility for it. Don't try to hide it or pass it on to someone else. George Murray says, "Openly admit you were wrong, and make every effort to learn from the mistake. People usually respond to admitted fallibility."

A lot of damage can result when a leader is unwilling to admit an error. But Hans Finzel provides a good reminder: Human beings are not omniscient. "A big dose of humility goes a long way to making things right," he says. "I find that two of the most powerful words in a leader's arsenal are, 'I'm sorry.'"

Clyde Cook told an interesting story of a mistake he made while chancellor at Biola University. "I remember trying to change the academic calendar at Biola. It made perfect sense to me why we should make this change, but somehow my brilliant ideas were not communicated beyond the deans. When the faculty and the student body learned about this, there was a huge protest.

"A definition of leadership I have often found interesting is, 'A leader is a person who sees a parade and gets at the head of the line.' I relied on this definition to get me out of what could have been a dire predicament. I realized right away that I was not the leader in this particular situation because I had no followers. The so-called followers were all marching in a parade in a different direction. I abandoned my position and got to the head of their line!"

Second, *work with your people to make a change, and implement it.* Talk with the people who were affected by the mistake, and get their ideas. Involve your team in developing a new strategy. And then go ahead and boldly go out and, in the words of Marvin Schuster, "restart your engine."

Sam Chand says he handles failure much different than he did his early days, when he thought he "knew everything!" Now he simply says, "Oops! I messed up—let's try this again, differently."

When you can embrace mistakes—and even failures—you've opened the door for growth and a different outcome for the next time.

Notes on Leadership

Have you ever gone public with a program or direction only to discover that you were wrong? How did you handle it?

Steve Douglass

"Needless to say I have made plenty of mistakes—gratefully most of them privately. In my case my process is:

- *Verify that the decision was wrong.*
- *If it is wrong, start by admitting that to myself. If it was my mistake, I need to "own" the error.*
- *Next involve the right people in taking the change public— those most affected, and key influencers.*
- *Communicate: with humility and repentance (if appropriate), with concern for the inconvenience (or worse) involved; with clarity."*

Joe Stowell

"Humbly ask for forgiveness. Examine what caused you to misfire—i.e., not enough counsel, not knowing your people, too much 'ready, fire, aim'? Learn from the experience and know that if you handle it correctly, that you'll live to serve again."

Bruce Fong

"Be quick to apologize when wrong. Admit error without pride. Theologically, Satan uses pride as a weapon against leaders. No use letting him have his way in our lives."

Steve Farrar

"All I know to do is to admit the mistake and clean up your mess as best you can. If trust has been lost, it will take time to get it back. With others, you may never regain trust."

Sheila Bailey

"I handled it by:

- *Using various approaches such as refocusing on the purpose; the need; the people; the timing of the program; the planning time; the budget and the facilities.*
- *Listening to constructive criticism.*
- *Making a U-turn and going another route.*
- *Approaching the person who was the hindrance.*
- *Sharing my concern with a team member(s).*
- *Casting the vision to ensure that people have embraced the vision. Allowing them time to ask questions and give suggestions.*
- *If there is opposition, determine if it is a battle worth fighting."*

Ric Cannada Jr.

"Many times we have launched programs that were not effective or at least did not continue to be effective. I learned early to be willing to change, to stop doing something, to be willing to keep trying new programs and new ways in order to find something effective. I have not been hesitant to admit that something is not working and we need to do something different."

"Humble yourselves, therefore, under the mighty hand of God so that at the proper time he may exalt you."

＊1 PETER 5:6

"Rejoice to renew your surrender to Him. Come, in poverty of spirit, to be led by the Spirit that is of God."

＊ANDREW MURRAY

CHAPTER SIX

SEASONS OF
BROKENNESS

I have a friend who was proud of the fact that he almost never fell. By that, I mean he went over twenty years without losing his footing and falling to the ground—even while running or walking on icy streets and sidewalks. "I might slip, but I always recover," he would say. "I can't remember the last time I fell."

That lasted until the day he ran out to his car in a parking lot just after a torrential downpour. Suddenly he was on his back, with one of his legs in searing pain.

His left knee was surgically repaired, but six years have passed, and he still feels the effects of that fall every day. He feels the knee with every step he takes, and has difficulty standing in one place for more than five minutes. Today he considers his weak knee a living reminder of the truth of 1 Corinthians 10:12, which says, "Therefore let anyone who thinks that he stands take heed lest he fall."

"For all those years, I had other problems with my body, but I could always brag about my coordination," he says, "and all I was really doing was setting myself up for a big fall! I think I needed to be reminded that I am not the one who is ultimately in control of my life."

God has a way of doing that—letting us know that life is not about us . . . that we are not the one in control. God will do whatever it takes to remind us that there is never a single second in our lives when we can make it on our own. So He takes us through seasons and episodes of brokenness to keep us under His shadow and to tie our hearts to His. And in order for Him to trust us, sometimes He has to break us.

A FALL WAITING TO HAPPEN

I think this is especially true in the lives of those whom God has called into leadership. Because of the insistent, perpetual pull we feel toward pride, we find ourselves having to crucify our flesh and intentionally dismantling pride's mastery over our lives and our choices. If we don't do it, God will. As author Randy Alcorn writes:

> When we start thinking we're special, that we've earned people's respect, that we have a lot to offer, then we become proud. That means that God is opposed to us, and we are operating outside the grace that He only gives to the humble. That makes us a fall waiting to happen: "Pride goes before destruction and a haughty spirit before a fall" (Proverbs 16:18).
>
> God knows the hearts of leaders. If we are in this for fame, money or power over people (including the power of ego-feeding and

sexual seduction), God knows and He will bring His hand of judgment upon us. "It is a dreadful thing to fall into the hands of the living God" (Hebrews 10:31).

But if we are broken, humble, quick to admit and confess our weaknesses and sins, He will shed His grace upon us, comfort us and empower us. Then, and only then, we will be Christ-like and Christ-exalting. Then, and only then, we will be leaders worth following.

I have seen this at work in my own life, especially during the early years of my ministry. The combination of a few early successes and a little recognition can make a young man feel as if he's a lot better than he really is and that the cause of Christ is really privileged to have what he has to offer. It doesn't take much to become intoxicated with yourself. So God introduces us to the cure for pride: a series of circumstances in which we get acquainted with pain and our inadequacy.

Monty Watson, a teaching pastor at Fellowship Bible Church in Roswell, Georgia, observes that, "Pride is innate and a dragon that must be slain . . . God breaks us at various times in our lives to raise us up to the next level. A brokenness episode in our thirties does not exempt us from a brokenness episode in our forties."

Pride is proprietary. It wants to own what belongs to God. Brokenness is God's way of showing us that He owns our lives and He gets the glory for what He does through us.

When Monty says that "God breaks us at various times to raise us up to the next level," he is referring to becoming more Christlike, more godly. This is the "next level" described by the apostle Paul in Philippians 3:7–10:

But whatever gain I had, I counted as loss for the sake of Christ. Indeed, I count everything as loss because of the surpassing worth of knowing Christ Jesus my Lord. For his sake I have suffered the loss of all things and count them as rubbish, in order that I may gain Christ and be found in him, not having a righteousness of my own that comes from the law, but that which comes through faith in Christ, the righteousness from God that depends on faith—that I may know him and the power of his resurrection, and may share his sufferings, becoming like him in his death.

A LIMP, NOT A STRUT

Seasons or episodes of brokenness will come in different forms for different leaders. They may be spurred by things out of our control—like illness, injury, unwarranted attacks by others, or choices made by children. God may discipline us for disobedience. He may allow us to feel the full consequences of sin.

Bruce Fong, president of Michigan Theological Seminary, says that mentors told him that painful moments would be inevitable in leadership. But he thought these moments "would be optional for me." They were not. "Opposition, division, gossip, accusations were all a part of the pain . . . These tender times are a rite of passage. Greater responsibility and leadership opportunities lie on the other side of such tests. It doesn't seem fair but it certainly seems to be the pattern that God uses."

Another friend calls a brokenness episode ten years ago "probably the singular most beneficial thing to happen to me as a leader. I vividly remember being in the shower and it was as if all of the air escaped from a balloon. I came to the end of myself and realized that I could no longer do it.

"That is exactly where God wanted me. He humbled me and that is what every leader needs. It is highly doubtful if God can ever use a man greatly until He hurts him deeply."

Sometimes a period of brokenness will catch us by surprise.

My friend Gary Rosberg, for example, went through a five-month period of depression following his father's death in 1996. It disrupted his life, his family, and his ministry as a counselor, author, and speaker. "God broke me so He could use me on the other side of the pain," Gary says today. "It stirred a greater sense of empathy and compassion for others. It has made me more sensitive toward the pain and hurt of others."

God wants everything that we do as leaders—and the way in which we do it—to reflect the image of His Son. This is our driving force, our holy aspiration in all things. But in order to get there, i.e., increasingly more of Him and less of us, He has to break us. Much like the shepherd who breaks the leg of the sheep that wanders off on its own, God breaks us so that we know that we are being carried by Him. And that is a sweet, wonderful, safe place to be.

This is why, in the words of Dr. Samuel Chand, "No leader walks with a strut—they always walk with a limp." It is during the seasons of brokenness that we encounter and "wrestle" with God and He marks our lives with a fresh sense of the reality that we *forever* need Him. We begin to understand and embrace in the deepest recesses of our souls that our need for God is not theoretical.

This is the lesson that the patriarch Jacob learned during a dark and lonely time in his life. He was overwhelmed with fear because he had to face his powerful brother, Esau, and the very real possibility of losing his life (Genesis 32). And there was good reason for his fear—Jacob had stolen Esau's birthright, the privileged position of the firstborn son (Genesis 27) and now he was staring at payday.

Then something strange happened. The night before the meeting, the angel of the Lord appeared to Jacob, and they wrestled all night long. It was during that struggle that "Jacob's hip was put out of joint" (Genesis 32:25). Jacob desperately wanted the angel of the Lord to bless him and he did (32:26–30). But the next morning when Jacob left town, he was "limping because of his hip" (32:31).

Don't miss this: *Jacob encountered God and left with a limp.* Those special times and seasons of struggle (brokenness episodes) leave us—dare I say it—wonderfully scarred. We are marked by God. And our "limp" is a reminder that we are human, frail, and weak. But it is also a monument to the grace, mercy, and power of God. Our "limp" is a trophy. It says that God carried us. It says that He is all that we need. He is our source, our strength, our everything.

HOLD TIGHT TO GOD

I have come to believe that a Christian leader's greatest mentor are the dark, lonely times in which God marks our souls with that profound sense of our need for Him. Perhaps as you read these words, you are right in the middle of a wrestling match with God. You feel as if God has taken you to the mat. You are being battered by circumstances, and you may be full of fear. You might be under some unusual attack by the devil or people being used by the devil. Maybe you're struggling with disappointment or discouragement.

Hold tight to God during this time. Even when you don't *sense* the affirmation of His presence, cling to Him. Absorb yourself in His Word and hold fast to His promises. Keep crying out to Him. Stay connected to and lean on your brothers and sisters in Christ. And by all means keep a journal nearby and write down your feelings and thoughts, especially the lessons God is teaching you.

Don't waste the spiritual equity; God is creating in you a greater capacity to know Him and to love Him more. You are learning what it really means to need Him. God loves it when we know that we need Him. This "limp" is your core credential as a leader.

You are not alone. This is God's pattern and process. There are monumental wrestling matches in the life of every leader whom God would trust with His assignments. I think of Dwight L. Moody, when the Chicago Fire of 1871 destroyed the buildings that housed his ministries and the pressures and exhaustion he was experiencing (see *A Passion for Souls* by Lyle Dorsett). It was also during this time that God met with Moody in a powerful way. Throughout the remainder of his life, Moody would point back to that season as the time in which he learned what it meant to depend on God.

Charles Haddon Spurgeon, who some consider to be the greatest preacher of all time, struggled with physical pain and depression throughout much of his adult life and ministry. In the preface to his wonderful little devotional *Checque Book of the Bank of Faith*, Spurgeon writes:

> *I have been cast into waters to swim in, which, but for God's upholding hand, would have proved waters to drown in. I have endured tribulations from many flails. Sharp bodily pain succeeded mental depression . . . The waters rolled in continually, wave upon wave . . . I have traversed those oceans which are not Pacific full many a time: I know the roll of the billows, and the rush of the winds. Never were the promises of Jehovah so precious to me as at this hour. Some of them I never understood till now; I had not reached the date at which they matured, for I was not myself mature enough to perceive their meaning.*

I'm thinking, too, about the young leader who sat in my office and told me about a series of embarrassing failures he had recently gone through. He said to me in so many words that he wanted to go run and hide. But he couldn't. He had to face the people he had let down, and he had to grapple with deep feelings of inadequacy and incompetence. He wanted to walk away but he didn't. He felt in his heart that the Lord wanted him to trust Him through the most difficult thing that he has faced so far.

Then he opened his journal and began reading to me the sweet, precious insights God was teaching him during this dark hour. These were lessons on depending on God and expressions of this young man's profound need for God to meet him in his darkness.

A SONG OF DESPERATION

I don't know of any leader who has not spent time in the parched barren desert of brokenness. The "withholding" is necessary to create in us a desperation, a longing for the presence and sustaining power of God. That's what the sons of Korah describe in Psalm 42:1–3.

Bible scholars believe that Psalm 42 was written while King David was on the run because his son Absalom was coming after him to kill him. The worship leaders, the sons of Korah, wrote a song of desperation, of brokenness: "As a deer pants for flowing streams, so pants my soul for you, O God. My soul thirsts for God, for the living God. When shall I come and appear before God? My tears have been my food day and night, while they say to me continually 'Where is your God?'"

The picture is compelling. Just like a deer that is out of place in the desert where there is no water, so David and his loyal friends were out of place. They needed God desperately. And I believe God *wanted* David to be in this place. Why? So he would know with every fiber of his being that his deepest need is always and forever God.

I believe God uses brokenness as a tool to prepare you for the assignments He has for you. Brokenness is God's way of adding weight, supernatural substance to your life and the assignments He gives to you. If you don't have this sense of your inadequacy and His all-sufficiency, you will lead with your own resources and abilities. You will lose the awareness of your need.

But once you've been through a season of brokenness, God is able to use you in greater ways than ever before. Joe Stowell, for example, says that brokenness "has provided a sense of empathy and patience with the frailties of life and the challenges that those who are following me face."

Clyde Cook said that brokenness produces "a fellowship with the Lord Jesus Christ that cannot be experienced any other way." It also allows us to comfort and understand others who are experiencing brokenness. Paul writes, "Blessed be the God and Father of our Lord Jesus Christ, the Father of mercies and God of all comfort, who comforts us in all our affliction, so that we may be able to comfort those who are in any affliction, with the comfort with which we ourselves are comforted by God" (2 Corinthians 1:3–4).

What God allows you to experience—seasons of challenge and brokenness—produces a compassion that can sense and feel what others may be experiencing. Your brokenness pulls you toward others who are in need. You become a source of hope and encouragement for them. Through your pain and weakness, others are made whole.

SINCERE REPENTANCE

I should note here that a broken leader will only be useful to others when he or she truly draws close to God. Especially when the brokenness involves a level of sin that may require removal from public ministry. God does restore fallen leaders. But restoration always follows sincere repentance.

Not long ago it was discovered that a well-known Christian leader had been living a secret life. The news was devastating to those who knew him or knew of him. My heart went out to him because apparently he felt trapped and he had struggled with this particular weakness for years. But I was a bit disturbed when, during an interview, another Christian leader commented that this man would be a more compassionate, sympathetic leader because of what he has just been through and that he should be forgiven and "restored to leadership."

That gave me pause, because I felt the sentiment was premature. Before any talk of restoration, there should be a demonstration of the fruit of repentance. Once again, leadership is a sacred trust and when a leader sins, he has not only sinned against God but he has also violated the trust given to him by those who love him and are influenced by him.

Just as leadership is not a private, personal matter, so the results and ramifications of sin go far beyond the boundaries of your personal world—it has an impact on your spouse, your children, those you led to Christ and discipled as well as those who have been affected by your choices and decisions.

A wise older pastor was asked one day when is it appropriate to restore someone who has sinned. His response was priceless: "When the repentance is known as broadly as the sin."

THE MIND-SET OF A GODLY LEADER

The Bible says that "God opposes the proud, but gives grace to the humble" (James 4:6). Think about that. God actually comes after the self-reliant (the proud) and gives His favor (grace) to the humble.

It pleases God when you demonstrate that you need Him. This is the attitude, the mind-set, of a godly leader. You run from pride and intentionally live and lead from a posture of dependence on Him.

That's the only place to be. God's assignments involve changed lives, and He can only use you if your life has been yielded to Him.

I like this thought from Tim Kimmel. "If a leader doesn't humble himself, he leaves God no choice but to humiliate him. And He will because He must. The work of His kingdom cannot be left at the mercy of a leader who is wrapped up in himself."

UNCOMMON
COMMUNION

"But we have this treasure in earthen vessels, so that the surpassing greatness of the power will be of God and not from ourselves."

✳ 2 CORINTHIANS 4:7 NASB

"Why do so many workers break down? Not from overwork, but because there has been friction of the machinery; there hasn't been enough oil of the Spirit."

✳ D. L. MOODY

CHAPTER SEVEN

HIS RESOURCES

I'll never forget a conversation with a man who was discouraged because he wasn't seeing any growth or progress in his speaking ministry. If you looked at what this man had to offer, you would assume his ministry would be thriving. He was bright, educated, and admired by others. He was a creative and articulate speaker. He had a ton of contacts in the evangelical community. But it wasn't working out for him—he wasn't receiving the number of speaking engagements he expected, and he was worried about his finances.

As we talked over lunch, I sensed that the problem was that he was too aware of his gifts and experience. He assumed those were the key to success. He thought he had a lot to offer to God, and he couldn't understand why God was not blessing him.

This friend was typical of many disappointed and discouraged leaders I've met over the years. They can't understand why their ministries are not more successful. Haven't they paid their dues? Don't they have the same skills as other leaders? Why were they not more recognized?

I have come to conclude that the truly great, effective leaders are not always the "best" leaders. Let me explain. What we value the most will be the foundation upon which we build our leadership. If your primary calling card is the belief that your skills, education, and experience make you capable of fulfilling God's assignments for you, then you're in trouble.

In a certain sense, based on your background, you may in fact be the best qualified and, in comparison to others, the best leader. But when the source of your leadership is your personal competency, the contribution you make to the assignment God has given to you will—in the long run—be mediocre at best. You may shine for a season, but at some point you will begin to experience failure.

That's because God gives leaders assignments beyond their ability to accomplish. We're not capable of doing what He has called us to do. And that's the way it should be.

Education, experience, and training are important, and I would even say vital, to accomplishing the tasks God places before a leader. We must be committed to developing the gifts and talents God has given to us. But there is a problem when we view these things as *the reason* why God uses us and as *the source* of our effectiveness and success. In my view, too many of us are trusting in our competencies as the primary means for advancing the interests of His kingdom.

PLUMMET THE DEPTHS OF INTIMACY

Because your assignments are beyond your ability, and because you need to depend on God for guidance, wisdom, and power, everything you do as a distinctively Christian leader should emanate from your walk with God. I am drawn to the observation of Ric Cannada, president of Reformed Theological Seminary:

The leader's walk with God is crucial. The more responsibility I have been given, the more I have felt the need for God's grace and wisdom, and the more I have sought to carve out time to be alone with the Lord in the Word and in prayer . . . I sense my need for guidance and the Lord's blessings on my efforts that are so feeble and short-sighted and ineffective in themselves.

God not only delights in our need to come to Him for wisdom and grace, but He also *invites* us to come. I love that wonderful invitation in James 1:5: "If any of you lacks wisdom, let him ask God, who gives generously to all without reproach, and it will be given him." God wants to display His awesome wisdom and power through us. But we must come to Him to get it.

He is using what He has called us to do to not only accomplish the task but also to *call us to plummet the depths of intimacy with Him.* It is in those seasons of seeking Him and crying out to Him for His direction and solutions that we tap into His power and we cultivate a deep heart connection with the God of the assignment and the God of our souls.

This is what I call *uncommon communion.*

I'm not just referring to daily times of prayer and Bible study; I'm talking about something more. It is God leveraging the very assignment He has given to us to accelerate the leader's sanctification. It is allowing the enormity of the task—the awareness of what we don't know, what we don't have, and what we so desperately need—to drive us to be absorbed in His presence.

Phillips Brooks, the prominent nineteenth-century pastor, said it best: "Do not pray for tasks equal to your powers; pray for powers equal to your tasks. Then the doing of the work shall be no miracle, but you shall be a miracle." God's heart is that you and the assignment become demonstrations of His glory and power.

PERFORMANCE REVIEW

As I write these words, I am reminded of the vision that the Lord has placed on my heart and the hearts of the leaders of the church that I have the privilege of serving as senior pastor. These are bold, faith-sized plans that only God can pull off. We have been driven to our knees in dependence on God. But if we stop looking to the Lord for His wisdom, grace, and power, we will fall flat on our faces. Psalm 127:1 says, "Unless the Lord builds the house, those who build it labor in vain."

I also know what it's like to try to do God's work in my own strength. And I've seen the results of this futile endeavor in the lives of numerous friends and colleagues. I remember one friend who poured himself into planting a new church. But after three years of a relentless schedule and almost nonstop activity, he began to experience and exhibit classic signs of burnout—anger, crying for no apparent reason, the loss of motivation and joy, withdrawing from friends and even family. Unfortunately, such burnout is all too common in church-related leaders.

Through the love and intervention of friends, he was able to take some extended time off and get the help he needed. When he talks about that dark time in his life, he observes that it wasn't that his work, his assignment, was off base—that was very right, and it was of God. His problem was a performance orientation that caused him to assume the responsibility for the ministry that only belonged to God. Instead of relinquishing the burdens and challenges to the Lord, he took them into his own hands to fix, and this crushed him.

The church he leads is dynamic and growing. But he has learned to cast his burdens on the Lord and to go to Him to get what he needs in order to do what God has called him to do. And he has become an extraordinarily effective leader.

THE OTHER "SNL"

My friend's experience echoes what Robertson McQuilkin observes: "A person with SNL (strong, natural, leader) characteristics can lead effectively, but only marginally accomplish God's purposes, which are spiritual in nature and require a close walk with the Spirit."

Throughout the Bible the unmistakable message that almost screams at us is that *God does it all.* His leaders draw a clear path between what's been accomplished through them and how it was done. God did it. I am reminded of God's words to Zerubbabel, "Not by might, nor by power, but by my Spirit, says the Lord of hosts" (Zechariah 4:6).

Let me ask you—whose strength are you tapping into to accomplish what you are called to do? How do you really operate? How do you approach the tasks and responsibilities before you? Do you suck it up, put your "game face" on, and remind yourself of how good you are and what you are capable of doing? Do you get by on the strength of your personality and willpower to make things happen?

If so, how is this working for you? Are you damaging any of your relationships? Is your family happy and healthy? How is your health—physical, emotional, and spiritual? How do the people who report to you feel about your leadership?

These are very important questions. God is making a statement about Himself through the leadership assignments He gives you. And He does not want you to pollute what He is doing by relying on a counterfeit source, namely, yourself.

This truth certainly doesn't mean you are totally passive in the process. But you take each step in a spirit of surrender and obedience; you commit to trusting and relying upon the Lord for His wisdom, strength, and direction each step of the way. In this wonderful sense you *participate* with God in doing the work He has placed in your hands. You lead from supernatural resources.

Never underestimate the power of self-deception and the pull toward self-reliance. Apart from the presence and power of God, these are irresistible. Do not trust yourself. Respond to God's call to be your source for everything. If you don't, you will damage God's work by extracting Him from the very thing He initiated in the first place.

GO TO THE SOURCE

I should make it clear that I am not saying that education, training, and experience are irrelevant for leaders. Competency is a good thing. God's call for our lives demands our faithful development and the pursuit of excellence. It is not unspiritual to develop your mind and improve your skills to stay ahead of the challenges that we face in our calling as leaders.

In fact, Paul encouraged the young leader Timothy to be faithful in his growth and development. Take a look at Paul's instructions to Timothy:

> Command and teach these things. Let no one despise you for
> your youth, but set the believers an example in speech, in

conduct, in love, in faith, in purity. Until I come, devote yourself
to the public reading of Scripture, to exhortation, to teaching. Do
not neglect the gift you have, which was given you by prophecy
when the council of elders laid their hands on you. Practice these
things, devote yourself to them, so that all may see your progress.
✳ 1 TIMOTHY 4:11–15

Clearly the apostle Paul was exhorting Timothy to not only
grow in his walk with God but to also grow and develop in the
area of his ministry competencies. God wants us to be faithful
and responsible stewards concerning the gifts and opportunities
before us. No doubt about it—we need to be the best that we
can be.

But again the key word is *source*. No matter how gifted and
competent we are, we cannot sustain spiritual impact and honor
God by relying on the arm of flesh. As we have seen, that's why
the very nature of God's assignments for us is beyond what we
naturally have. God uses these assignments to call us back to Him,
our eternal source.

BECOMING *AND* DOING

There's one more reason for staying connected to God and
depending upon His resources. *God is using what He has given you
to do to not only accomplish His assignments but to make you what
He wants you to become.* Think about that for a second. It's important that you do not separate God's assignments and God's
character-building program. This is at the core of your relationship with Him. He is using what He has called you to do to make
us more like His Son and to prove Himself faithful to you.

The wealth and richness of your life and leadership over time
is produced by the consistent habit of turning to God in the face

of your weaknesses, difficulties, storms, and seemingly insurmountable challenges, and seeing Him unfailingly come through time and again. Over time this experience produces in your heart that delightfully strange and wonderful combination of humility and profound confidence that the God of the ages will give you what you need and do everything He promised when you turn away from yourself and trust Him completely. I am reminded of what David said in Psalm 31:19: "Oh, how abundant is your goodness, which you have stored up for those who fear you and worked for those who take refuge in you, in the sight of the children of mankind."

FOUR JEWELS

I am indebted to Dr. Henry Blackaby for his book *Spiritual Leadership*, in which he writes of the different factors God uses to mature a Christian leader. I call them the "four jewels" of leadership development. These four jewels are precious—they are to be treasured because they keep driving us back to God for His strength and power. They are tools that God uses to make us more like Christ.

These four jewels all have to do with what would be considered the unpleasant, hard stuff of life. They are the experience of every follower of Jesus Christ but in a particular sense they are characteristic of distinctively Christian leaders. They are not the experiences we would choose on our own. But I have come to strongly agree that these four developmental experiences are not only necessary in the life of a Christian leader, but they also will be repeated throughout the course of our lives.

These four topics come from Dr. Blackaby, but the explanations and applications are mine:

The first jewel is *suffering*. Every person God will trust with influencing others will suffer. You cannot talk about the ability of

God to comfort others and to sustain them through times of suffering and pain unless you have been there yourself (2 Corinthians 1:3–7).

Suffering makes your heart tender and open. You know what it's like to feel alone, confused, and in pain. You also know what it is like to be carried by God when you were out of strength and too weak to take the next step (Psalm 28:8–9). When you experience trials such as the loss of a child or a spouse, physical pain, a life-threatening illness, or attacks and bitter accusations from others, God allows you the privilege of identifying with His Son, the Lord Jesus (Philippians 1:29).

Suffering is God's call to take refuge in Him, to run to Him for shelter and protection from the gale force winds that threaten to destroy you (Psalm 31:3–5). You are then able to say with a profound sense of identification and authenticity, "God is our refuge and strength, a very present help in trouble" (Psalm 46:1). You know what it means to be met by God in your dark times.

The second jewel is *personal struggles.* This is closely related to suffering and perhaps it should be considered as such. But this is the stuff that you repeatedly wrestle with because it won't go away. It's that "thorn in the flesh" (see chapter 4) that keeps you coming back to God for His strength and encouragement to keep fighting the ongoing battle. It may be like the depression that the great preacher C. H. Spurgeon struggled with his entire adult life. Or the lust that literally keeps a friend of mine on his face before God every day. Maybe it's the plague of pleasing people that I have struggled with throughout the course of my life and ministry. Perhaps it's an overbearing personality that you constantly have to rein in because of your tendency to hurt and alienate others, even the people you love. Or maybe it's the voice in your ear that keeps whispering to you that you're not good enough.

The third jewel is *failure*. It's a dangerous thing to follow a leader who has never failed. Let's be honest: Anyone who claims to have never failed has a character problem—lying.

There is something to the old line that "failure is the back door to success." Failure produces humility and an appropriate caution to ensure you are not only doing what God is leading you to do, but you are also doing it the way He wants it done.

Unexamined failure teaches you nothing. In fact, it can throw you into discouragement and depression, not to mention the stupidity of continuing to do the wrong thing. This happened to me in 1997. I gave leadership to a national conference that came far short of meeting our attendance goal for the event. We lost a lot of money and I was left with the challenge of raising the funds to cover the deficit. I was embarrassed and discouraged. In fact, for me emotionally it was one of the lowest points of my ministry.

It wasn't until I sat down and faced the painful reality of the wrong assumptions I had made that I began to embrace the lessons that the Lord wanted to teach me through that experience. Every leader has to occasionally wipe the egg off his face and say, "That wasn't fun. But what can I learn from this?"

I hope I am not coming across unduly negative, but I am persuaded that failure is a vital part of leadership. In fact, with rare exception most of the great leaders in the Bible have been marked by failure. It's part of the journey. Failure is God's glaring object lesson that says, "Check out what happens when you do things your way." Let's aim to have the humility and the sense to learn the lesson and do it His way.

The fourth jewel is *success through hardship*. Leadership was never meant to be easy. The very word, leadership, implies the willingness to take others to a place where none of you has been before. In our context, it is following God's call to a new reality.

In a sense leadership is the unexpected, the difficult. Leadership is the ability to endure. There can be no leadership apart from adversity and hard times. Your credibility to lead is in direct relationship to your ability to endure. This was the sage advice given by the apostle Paul to the young leader Timothy. Look at these words:

> You then, my child, be strengthened by the grace that is in Christ Jesus, and what you have heard from me in the presence of many witnesses entrust to faithful men who will be able to teach others also. Share in suffering as a good soldier of Christ Jesus. No soldier gets entangled in civilian pursuits, since his aim is to please the one who enlisted him. An athlete is not crowned unless he competes according to the rules. It is the hard-working farmer who ought to have the first share of the crops. Think over what I say, for the Lord will give you understanding in everything.
> 2 TIMOTHY 2:1–7

Soldiers, athletes, and farmers have to work hard and endure before they experience victory or reap the harvest. As a leader, the hardships you endure are part of your development as a leader and follower of Jesus Christ. There is indeed a price to be paid to do what God has called you to do. But the hardships produce eternal fruit and blessing far beyond anything you can imagine.

Jim Reese says one of the most difficult times in his business career was when, at the age of thirty, "I was responsible for the success or closing of the Maxwell House Coffee plant in Jacksonville. I can remember walking in every day feeling so responsible, and because of that heavy responsibility and the facing of knowing I couldn't do it on my own, my dependence was so clear."

Jim says he looks back on this experience and recognizes that God gave him skills and resources way past his capability in order to complete the task. "I cried out and moved and walked with a confidence not in myself but in Him that I would do my best, that I would listen closely, and I would work to use all the skills that He had given me to do all I could do."

THE "STORY BEHIND THE STORY"

As Jim learned, God gives you the strength to complete His assignments. As you press into God to do His will, you become His will.

As a distinctively Christian leader, what you do is really a statement about God's sufficiency and power. When He brings painful reminders into your life of your desperate need for Him, treasure these reminders as wonderful gifts of His love and grace.

When I visit other leaders, I enjoy looking at the things they choose to display in their office—the pictures, the awards and plaques, memorabilia commemorating milestones and accomplishments. I often ask these individuals for the "story behind the story" of some of the objects, and I've discovered that often what they value about the honor or the recognition is not what you might think.

Certainly they appreciate being noticed, but usually they were not expecting this recognition. More often than not they were responding to what was in front of them with faith and obedience. The recognition found them.

No, what they really treasure is the memory of the lessons from the journey—the difficulties they endured, the price they had to pay, and the way they grew closer to Christ in the process of "getting there."

At this stage of the game I've got some of that stuff on the shelves and walls of my office as well. These are daily reminders of what God has done and the valleys He has walked me through.

He is our everlasting source!

Notes on Leadership

What are some of the things younger leaders need to be careful of regarding the relationship between pride and their influence as a leader?

Monty Watson

"Younger leaders, and I think I was guilty of this twenty years ago too, tend to rely on new thinking and new ideas to the point and assume depth and maturity of thinking. 'New' cannot replace substance, depth, and maturity. I see younger leaders quick to dismiss older leaders as obsolete rather than glean from leaders with more experience in the game."

Steve Farrar

"Young leaders have a tendency to rely on their gifts. We tend to identify early where we are strong and capable. Certain things come easy to us because we are gifted. That's where pride must be watched like a hawk."

Tim Kimmel

"The sooner a young Christian leader figures out that God has given Him the job of humbling himself, the sooner God will be able to hand more responsibility to that leader. If a leader doesn't humble himself, he leaves God no choice but to humiliate him. And He will because He must. The work of His kingdom cannot be left at the mercy of a leader who is wrapped up in himself."

Steve Douglass

"Pride is not good in any setting—leadership or otherwise. Especially with younger, less mature leaders. I advise not to think too highly of yourself."

Ric Cannada

"Pride will make others not want to follow you over the long haul, and will cause you to stumble at some point badly in what you do or the attitudes you display and discourage and dishearten those who follow you."

Marvin Schuster

"Pride can be seen by others, when you cannot recognize this sin, which also carries a stench of arrogance."

Ken Behr

"Pride is one of the easiest ways for a younger leader to lose their influence. Pride tells us 'we can do' while we need to understand that the wisdom that is needed is godly. Pride will also stop us from seeking others' advice and will often lead to quick, rash decisions and subpar results."

Jim Reese

"One of the most important areas for all leaders, but especially young leaders, is the ability to continuously learn. Pride usually stops learning because the need to learn is many times not there. You can either feel you have arrived and thus don't need to learn, or because of your pride you are more concerned about how you look and sound than what you are doing or learning!"

George Murray

"Younger leaders need to respect and listen to age and experience, regardless of the title or position of the older, more experienced person. Younger leaders also need to be sensitive to the perception that others have of them. Often younger leaders are perceived by others as being cocky. In the eyes of the beholder, perception is reality."

Don Carson

"Pride in a young leader has the potential for doing damage of different kinds. It may corrode the leader's own heart . . . it may unnecessarily alienate the best of other people . . . some followers will simply ape this young leader and think, wrongly, that leadership ought to be arrogant, and thus become like him. When the Lord is not honored in one's Christian leadership, one is risking a much higher likelihood of generating spurious conversions, slightly twisted followers, and so forth."

Bruce Fong

"One mentor told me to never slip into the mode of believing my press clippings. Faithfulness to the Lord supersedes human acclaim."

"Seek the Lord and his strength; seek his presence continually!"

✳ PSALM 105:4

"Everything in my life is knitted together in His masterful way. My personal walk is not separate from my leadership. This integration keeps any leadership success in good balance. It is not spectacular success; it is simply obedience on my part and blessing on His part."

✳ DR. BRUCE FONG

CHAPTER EIGHT

HIS PRESENCE

Some years ago I took my son Bryndan with me on a speaking engagement at a Promise Keepers men's conference in Tampa, Florida. That evening, with my son in the audience, I spoke on moral purity. I encouraged the men to resist sexual temptation and, if they were married, to be faithful in keeping the marriage covenant.

When we returned to the hotel, Bryndan, who was a teenager at the time, asked me these two questions: "Dad, have you ever been tempted to cheat on Mom?" and "Why didn't you do it?"

I told my son that God in His grace has protected me through the years. I also told him that as a man I have fought sexual temptation and God has given me the strength to resist.

I shared that I often think of how much my wife and children love and trust me. "I carry you guys with me wherever I go."

But even more important, I told him, was my continual awareness of God's presence in my life. "God often brings to my mind who He is and what He has done for me and our family. He loves me and He has revealed Himself to me and He is with me. I don't want to do anything to hurt the heart of God."

God is with us and He wants us to be aware of His presence. That may come across as a simple statement, even a given. But wait! His presence is everything. The fact that *God Himself is with us* determines, alters, and changes how we live our lives and how we approach His business.

Do you realize the breadth and magnitude of the fact that God is with you? It's more than a sense of accountability for your actions and choices. It's more than an awareness of God as a compassionate and unconditional lover of your soul who tenderly meets you at your point of need. Praise God, He does love you and He is compassionate and merciful, coming to you in ways that profoundly identify with your pain and suffering.

But the God who says He is with you is also sovereign, holy, and just. He is the Ancient of Days and the Creator of the universe. He is the Sustainer and judge of mankind. All that He is and all that He has is wrapped up in His presence—His power, grace, love, mercy, holiness, strength, and wisdom. When you have Him, you have it all. To realize that God's presence is with you is a staggering, incomprehensible reality. That realization should cause you to fall on your face in worship.

HE IS HERE, HE IS WITH US

The presence of God is wonderfully addictive. King David said in Psalm 34:8, "Oh, taste and see that the Lord is good!

Blessed is the man who takes refuge in him!"

Obviously, when something is good, you typically want to go back for more. Karen and I have been married now for more than thirty-seven years. Our children are grown and no longer at home. Karen and I do a lot together. I cannot find the words to describe what it means to me to have her by my side, to know that she is with me. Sometimes when we are at home relaxing, I look across the room and see her and I smile because of her reassuring presence. Every Sunday when I stand to preach, I look out in the audience and see her and I know that she is with me—she's praying for me; we're doing this together. We love being with each other. Through these years our love for each other has grown deeper and sweeter.

How much more we should long for and glory in the presence of our great God! Hasn't He proved to be everything to us? Where would we be without Him? What could we do without Him? He loves us and He gives us challenges and assignments to keep us tied to His presence and His loving heart. How He wants to reveal Himself in us and through what He has called us to do.

When a leader seeks uncommon communion, his life will be marked by experiences that are anchor events, milestones that permanently mark his soul. These are historic encounters with God that we never forget. God comes to us often in dramatic ways and touches our lives. We are exposed to and experience an awesome sense of His presence. He gives us a fresh vision of Himself and often through these encounters come a new mission, a new assignment from Him. And always there is the assurance of His presence. We are overwhelmed with the realization that *He is here, He is with us.*

This has happened to me several times throughout my life and ministry. I remember as a teenager going to a local park to pray after school. God met me in those times alone with Him. It was during those prayer times that I first sensed that God wanted me to preach and teach His Word. As I read His Word and talked to Him, He filled my heart with a sense of confidence that He would use me and that He was with me.

Through the years, I've observed that before God makes clear to me what He wants me to do, I often experience a time or season of renewal in my heart. This happened just a few weeks ago. While ministering at a conference, I experienced a refreshing sense of personal revival. For weeks prior to that time, I had been struggling with how to handle some challenges our church faces. How sweet it was to experience the assurance that the Lord is with me! These are confirmations, reminders that He is with me. (I have learned, however, that what is important is to seek Him and not the experience. God doesn't always work the same way or manifest Himself in the same way.)

MOSES' ENCOUNTER WITH GOD LEAVES ITS MARK

Exodus 33 describes a classic, moving encounter that Moses had with God. At the time, Moses and the Israelites had been camped at Mount Sinai for many days. This was an extraordinary, dramatic time—the word "crisis" doesn't even begin to describe it. While Moses was on the mountain communing with God and receiving His instructions for the people, Aaron, whom he left in charge, allowed the people to run roughshod over him (Exodus 32:1–6). They were completely out of control, reverting back to idolatry and immorality.

Now we come to Exodus 33. God said it was time to leave Sinai and reembark on the journey to the land of promise (Exodus 33:1). Moses was rattled by the profound disobedience and rebellion of the people. He needed a special touch from God—the assurance deep in his innermost being that God was with him and with the people. Read carefully and closely this passionate plea from the heart of a leader for God's presence (Exodus 33:12–23):

Moses said to the Lord, "See, you say to me, 'Bring up this people,' but you have not let me know whom you will send with me. Yet you have said, 'I know you by name, and you have also found favor in my sight.' Now therefore, if I have found favor in your sight, please show me now your ways, that I may know you in order to find favor in your sight. Consider too that this nation is your people."

And he [God] said, "My presence will go with you, and I will give you rest," and he [Moses] said to him, "If your presence will not go with me, do not bring us up from here. For how shall it be known that I have found favor in your sight, I and your people? Is it not in your going with us, so that we are distinct, I and your people, from every other people on the face of the earth?"

And the Lord said to Moses, "This very thing that you have spoken I will do, for you have found favor in my sight, and I know you by name." Moses said, "Please show me your glory." And he said, "I will make all my goodness pass before you and will proclaim before you my name 'The Lord.' And I will be gracious to whom I will be gracious, and will show mercy on whom I will show mercy. But," he said, "you cannot see my face, for man shall not see me and live." And the Lord said, "Behold, there is a place by me where you shall stand on the rock, and while my glory passes by I will put you in a cleft of the rock, and I will cover you with my hand until I have passed by. Then I will take away my hand, and you shall see my back, my face shall not be seen."

HUNGERING AND WALKNG

There are four things to learn about God's presence and leadership from this amazing encounter.

First, *the challenges of leadership are meant to make you hungry for God.* There's an old saying—"We turn to God when our foundations are shaking only to discover it is God who is shaking them!"

Moses was shaken to the core. God was all Moses had and all Moses wanted. As leaders we need to pray that God will use the pressures that we face to give us an insatiable hunger and thirst for Him. This is a marvelous place to be. The more you hunger for Him, the closer He is to you. When you cry, "God, I need You," He answers, "I am right here, you have Me."

This is an incredible spiritual paradox. You are only filled with Him when you are desperate for Him. As Jeremiah 29:13 (NASB) tells us, "You will seek Me and find Me when you search for Me with all your heart."

Are the challenges you face producing in you despair, or are they causing you to be spiritually desperate? There is a big difference. Despair means to be without hope. Spiritual desperation means to turn to God as your only hope (Psalms 20:7; 25:2; 56:3–4). Often God turns up the heat until you feel your hunger and embrace your desperation.

Christian leader Joe Stowell reminds us that "being called to ministry puts all of us way beyond ourselves and leaves us with a healthy sense of insecurity and insufficient capacity to live up to the responsibilities. Which, in turn, thrusts us on Jesus to help us with the wisdom and discernment that we need to do His work. This required closeness to Him lets us experience Him in ways that make Him real to us and in turn real to our people." I remember once asking Bill Bright how he kept it all together. His responsibilities were enormous. I will never forget his response. He said, "If I took my eyes off of the Lord, I would be a dead man. But I have learned to place all of my concerns on Him and He gives me peace and the power to do what He has called me to do."

Second, *God's presence is the distinguishing characteristic of your leadership.* This is the battleground when it comes to distinctively Christian leadership. This demonstrates whether you are using a few Scripture quotations as a thin veneer over a worldly approach to leadership, or whether you are leading from His initiative and in light of His presence. In other words, what separates you from the pack is not your ability and proficiency in the art and skill of leadership—it is the call and obvious presence of God in your life.

Look again at what Moses says in Exodus 33:16: "For how shall it be known that I have found favor in your sight, I and your people? Is it not in your going with us, so that we are distinct, I and your people, from every other people on the face of the earth?" Basically, Moses said in so many words, "God, You are our statement!" He did not want to be like everybody else. He understood the unique nature of his mission.

Of course, you have not been called to deliver people from slavery and usher them into the Land of Promise. But if you are a follower of Jesus Christ and you sense that God has given you an assignment, then He wants to be central to how you approach and implement that assignment. He is your uniqueness and distinguishing characteristic!

The challenge you face as a leader is to intentionally acknowledge God's presence as you go about doing what He has called you to do. Although I am grateful for the many Christian resources available to us on how to be better leaders and how to be more effective and efficient in getting things done, from some of what I've read I sometimes get a sense that God is taken for granted. It almost feels as though some leaders are a little embarrassed to lead too much with God. It's as if their approach is, "Well, of course we know that God is with us. But it's up to us to figure out what we should do and how we should lead."

God doesn't want you to ignore Him or keep Him hidden as we exercise our leadership and do our work. That's why Bruce Fong says, "Everything in my life is knitted together in a masterful way. My personal walk is not separate from my leadership. That integration keeps any leadership success in good balance. It is not spectacular success; it is simply obedience on my part and blessing on His part."

As I watched Bill Bright, I observed that he did not separate what God called him to do from his walk and relationship with God. In fact, sitting in a meeting with him was like being in a prayer meeting. When issues and challenges came up, he would often stop without warning and pray aloud for God's wisdom. Or if there was a good report or an accomplishment, he would pause to thank and praise God for what He had done.

By making prayer a natural part of these meetings, he modeled to us younger leaders what it means to lead from God's presence. Certainly he was a man on a mission and he wanted to get things done. But along the way he had learned that, if leadership is all about God, then let's make it all about God.

Now I am aware that some of you reading these words are not in a position to publicly approach things the way Bill Bright did. And that's fine. Don't miss the point: What's most important is the attitude and heart commitment to live and operate from the presence of God. I'm not so sure that Daniel, a Jew, had public prayer times as he gave significant leadership to the Babylonians, who didn't follow the Lord God. But we know that he lived in and operated from God's presence (Daniel 1:8; 5; 6).

How connected you are to God's presence eventually will be seen in how you fulfill His assignments. In the words of Monty Watson, "It's always humbling when I preach how exposed my spiritual life really is. The Christian leader's walk with God is always on display."

Living in God's presence is everything to the Christian leader. I have a statue of a man on his knees in my office; he is bowed across a chair in prayer. Often when I look at that statue, the Lord reminds me that, in a sense, my full-time job is to live in His presence, cultivating intimacy with Him. This was the message that King David gave to his son Solomon in 1 Chronicles 28:9: "And you, Solomon my son, know the God of your father and serve him with a whole heart and a willing mind, for the Lord searches all hearts and understands every plan and thought. If you seek him, he will be found by you, but if you forsake him, he will cast you off forever."

A call to lead is a call to know God. Please do not miss this: A call to lead is a call to know God. Everything you do as a leader is an extension of the presence and the work of God in your life. Jim Reese puts it this way: "If I look at my life and my walk with God, it is so clear that my most effective times in business and in ministry are when I am close to God."

RESTING AND MOVING

The third truth we learn from Moses' encounter with God is that *God's presence causes you to lead from rest.* In Exodus 33:14, God said to Moses, "My presence will go with you, and I will give you rest." This could very well be a reference to the recent turmoil and upheaval caused by the rebellion of the people at Sinai. And God was specifically promising Moses a reprieve from the hassles. But I also think this is a reference to the peace and rest found in His presence.

Despite what is going on all around you, know that He not only has everything that you need, but He is also *giving* you all that you need to deal with whatever is before you. In this regard you operate from a tremendous position of strength, because His resources are endless. He gives you the strength to not just continue but to thrive. That's what Isaiah 40:29–31 is all about: "He gives power to the faint, and to him who has no might he increases strength. Even youths shall faint and be weary, and young men shall fall exhausted; but they who wait for the Lord shall renew their strength; they shall mount up with wings like eagles; they shall run and not be weary; they shall walk and not faint."

Best-selling author and Christian leader Randy Alcorn poignantly shares the relationship between his calling and his profound need for God's abiding presence:

Much of my life is invested in writing. In long lonely hours of writing, in the middle of the night, I have often asked God, "Is it worth it?" and He has gently reassured me it is. This happened regularly when I wrote my book Heaven. *I have repeatedly experienced His grace and kindness when I've called out to Him . . . and a great sense of discouragement when I haven't. In these challenging times, Jesus has truly showed Himself to be my best friend, not just in theory, but in reality. Not only do I call upon Him to help me accurately handle His Word when writing nonfiction, I ask Him for ideas and direction to craft quality stories in my fiction writing. He is the Creator, the Genius, the Master Storyteller, and I want to be a reflection of Him, even a pale reflection. I want my words to be tools of His Spirit. Nothing's more thrilling than to hear people say that God has changed their lives through something I've written. If I imagined*

*that was because of my genius, it would make me proud. But because
I have repeatedly called upon Him for help in the process, when I
hear these stories, I am filled not with pride, but sheer amazement
and gratitude to Him.*

I love the line "In these challenging times, Jesus has truly
showed Himself to be my best friend, not just in theory, but in reality." Randy experiences the wonderful presence of our Savior
while engaged in fulfilling God's assignment for his life. This is the
way it should be.

Finally, *do not move if you're not sure God is with you.* The Word
of God, prayer, the confirming leading of the Holy Spirit, and the
insight of godly people is essential to knowing and experiencing
with confidence a sense of God's presence. Moses did not want to
risk leaving Sinai unless he knew for sure that God indeed was
with him and the people. There was just too much at stake.

In the same way, there is too much at stake in your life to do
God's work in the energy of the flesh and for your own recognition. When this happens, all you've accomplished will ultimately
come to nothing. Your works will burn (1 Corinthians 3:10–15).

And what if you're not sure that God is with you? Follow the
example of Moses: Seek God while you wait for it. As a dear friend
said to me years ago, "The only thing worse than waiting on the
Lord is wishing that you had!"

As leaders, let's ask God to give us a longing for His presence
. . . It's everything!

"I will instruct you and teach you in the way you should go; I will counsel you with my eye upon you."

✳ PSALM 32:8

"I ask God nearly every morning to show me the work He has for me on this day. Having come to this point late in my life, I do not presume that He has big plans for me but I am totally content to work at whatever level and in whatever area He has for me."

✳ BOB GERNDT

CHAPTER NINE

HIS DIRECTION

Leadership is fueled by a compelling sense of mission. What inspires us to take action is an irresistible picture of either what *should be done* or what *could be done*. We then focus our determination to make it happen. This is true of all leadership.

But there is more. Christian leadership is all about *doing what God wants done*. There is no leadership apart from a clear assignment from God. As we saw in the case of King Uzziah, one of the most dangerous things for a Christian leader to do is to make assumptions about what God wants done. He wants to tell us what He wants to do.

The closer we get to God's heart, the stronger our faith becomes. Our steps become more certain because He has spoken to us, because He discloses Himself and His plans for us.

For some of you, this may sound a bit mystical. Perhaps you struggle with whether or not God speaks to leaders today the same way He did to people in the Bible. Personally I don't know what God's voice sounds like. I have never heard a voice in my head that I recognized as being distinctively God's voice. But I know God has spoken to me.

Let me explain. God primarily speaks to us through His Word, the sixty-six books of the Bible. God's Word is His will. And He will never lead us to do anything that contradicts what is in the Bible. But He also leads us by His Spirit. He gives us assignments and opens doors for ministry and service. He gives us impressions and ideas. When we pray to know what He wants us to do, He shows us in many ways. Often it's a sense of conviction about a choice—that somehow you know it's the right thing to do, and then you experience His peace as you follow Him.

And He wants us to keep coming to Him so that He can tell us what He wants to do through us. God's pattern in the Scriptures is to tell His leaders just enough so that they can take the immediate steps of obedience. But He does not give them the details of His plan. Often He will provide a compelling picture of the future (vision) to call us to purpose and to inspire action. Whether it was the call of Abraham to leave his homeland and become the father of many nations . . . the call of Moses to deliver Israel and lead them to the Land of Promise . . . the call of Joshua to make Canaan a peaceful place for Israel to live . . . the call of the disciples to "make disciples of all the nations" . . . the call of Paul to plant and expand the church among the Gentiles . . . the pattern was the same. *Godly leaders act on what God clearly tells them to do and then they keep coming to Him when they don't know what to do next.*

WE TRUST HIM BECAUSE HE'S TRUSTWORTHY

God has demonstrated His faithfulness to me in amazing and humbling ways through the years. So much of what He has called me to do has been pioneering in nature. Whether it was church planting, radio, writing books, launching ministries, or the unique, wonderful church I pastor now, I can't think of a time in which I had everything I needed ahead of time to do what I believe the Lord wanted me to do. There were always surprises, lack, unanticipated challenges and changes, opposition, and walking into unknown and unchartered territory (at least for me!). I often struggled (and still do) between fear and faith.

One of God's assignments for me was to put on a conference in 1981 for students and laypeople. This was the first event of the kind I had organized. I was excited about the prospect of a couple thousand people coming together to learn about how they could be more effective for Christ. What I didn't anticipate was the opposition from pastors and leaders who were friends of mine. If I had known up front this was coming, I would have made some different decisions. But God knew what I would face, and I was forced to rely on Him as my source of direction, wisdom, and strength.

What the Lord has been teaching me through these years is that He not only wants to work through me, but He also wants to *make me* as He works through me. He wants me to expand my vision of Him, get lost in His presence, and stand in awe of His power and His glory. But this cannot be an academic exercise. It has to be in real life and in real time. It's one thing to host a seminar on what God can do. It's quite another story to share what He has done and what you have become as a result.

I firmly believe that this is one of the primary reasons why He doesn't tell us everything ahead of time. Besides, if we had all of the information up front and we knew what we would have to endure, we would be scared to death! The truth of the matter is, we can't handle what He has shown us to do. So we have to trust Him. God wants us to be driven to our knees, so He gives us impossible assignments with unanticipated twists and turns.

During his years of leadership with Campus Crusade for Christ, Bill Bright was often asked about his experience of receiving God's assignment to begin an organization that would be involved in helping fulfill the Great Commission. At the time, in 1951, he was a businessman and seminary student. "The night that God gave me the original vision, I was at home studying for a Greek exam," Bright said. "It wasn't the kind of situation that is conducive to visions. But God in a supernatural way seemed to open up my mind, to give me a vision that embraced the whole world. It was so intoxicating that I almost burst with joy. I wanted to shout the praises of God at the top of my voice."

Bright said he was confident that God would use him and others "to reach the multitudes of the world for whom Christ died." But God didn't reveal how it would be done.

"I often think of the vision that God gave me that night as the beginning strokes of a giant-size painting. Here is the canvas, and the artist puts the broad sweeps on it—the landscapes, the mountains. Later he fills in the details. Had God given me all of the details that night, I am sure I would have lost my sanity. I couldn't possibly have taken it. But he gave me what I could take, and that was an experience never to be forgotten."[3]

THE PRIVILEGE OF ENTERING THE PRESENCE OF GOD

Clyde Cook observed, "There is a close relationship between your walk with God and the assignment He has given you. He has made you and knows the gifts He has given you. In order to maximize your effectiveness, you need to be close to Him."

As leaders, we have to fight to maintain the discipline of regularly entering God's presence to commune with Him and to get His heart and mind concerning what He wants us to do and how He wants us to do it. There's too much at stake for us to do otherwise. God's assignments have eternal implications. It's not just about the excitement and satisfaction of finishing a task or making something happen; it's the story of an assignment from God to have a lasting impact on our lives.

This is not a game we are playing; it's not a hobby we take up on the weekends. We are not a bunch of self-improvement gurus peddling comfortable advice so we all can feel good about ourselves. Neither are we Christian celebrities basking in our accomplishments, sharing with others how they can be like us. No, we are servants of the Most High God desperate to know and committed to doing everything our Commander in Chief tells us to do. We passionately want to know what God wants us to do.

Moses was given the impossible, unimaginable assignment of delivering the Hebrews from their Egyptian slavery into God's Land of Promise. God revealed His plan each step of the way, but He did not give Moses much guidance ahead of time. Moses did not receive a massive volume detailing route, schedule, key personnel, organizational charts, rest areas, meals and supplies, battle plans, and contingencies. Instead, God orchestrated circumstances and events that forced Moses to return to Him, asking, "God, help me . . . Please show me what's next."

Throughout the book of Exodus, you see a continual pattern of resistance/cooperation, dilemma/resolution, crisis/solution, opposition/victory, confusion/clarity, judgment/mercy, need/supply. *And before every turnaround, you find Moses entering the presence of God to learn what needed to be done next.*

This is how God works. Planning is not wrong; setting goals is not wrong. But self-reliance *is* wrong. By the time we see Moses in chapter 33 of Exodus, he and the Israelites have been delivered from slavery in Egypt and are traveling to the land that God has promised to them. Moses has learned the importance of seeking God. Look at these words in Exodus 33:7–11:

> Now Moses used to take the tent and pitch it outside the camp, and he called it the tent of meeting. And everyone who sought the Lord would go out to the tent of meeting, which was outside the camp. Whenever Moses went out to the tent, all the people would rise up, and each would stand at his tent door, and watch Moses until he had gone into the tent. When Moses entered the tent, the pillar of cloud would descend and stand at the entrance of the tent, and the Lord would speak with Moses. And when all the people saw the pillar of cloud standing at the entrance of the tent, all the people would rise and worship, each at his tent door. Thus the Lord used to speak to Moses face to face, as a man speaks to his friend. When Moses turned again into the camp, his assistant Joshua the son of Nun, a young man, would not depart from the tent.

This text captures my heart. As leaders entrusted with His assignments, we are called regularly to the tent of meeting. And there are some lessons we can learn from these tent meetings. Let's look at four of them.

AT THE TENT MEETING

First, *this meeting with God was a habit.* The opening line of verse 7 says, "Now Moses used to take the tent . . . " This apparently wasn't an occasional meeting that he had with God. The broader context of the book of Exodus underscores the regular, consistent habit Moses had of meeting with God. Moses' life and the successful accomplishment of the mission depended on these meetings with God. He didn't know enough to be able to lead God's people on his own. This habit was everything to him. It was his lifeline. His hope. His source. His confidence. He had to meet with God.

What about you? Are you regularly and consistently meeting with God for Him to give you His power and wisdom to do what He has placed in your hands to do? It is tempting to cut short these meetings, but they are the most important appointments in your schedule. Without meeting with Him, you have no spiritual credentials to provide leadership for His cause and kingdom.

You can't afford to miss it. He's waiting to meet with you.

Second, *the meeting was held away from distractions.* The tent was pitched "outside the camp, far off from the camp . . . " Can you imagine the clamor, noise, distractions, and just the blizzard of busyness that two and a half million people could dump on a leader? There were unfinished projects, and no doubt people were waiting to meet with him about important matters. But Moses made a special effort to take his tent away from the distractions to a quiet place to meet with God.

When I made the transition from years of an itinerant ministry to being a senior pastor, I underestimated the number of distractions I would experience in a thriving church. I've always had a good work ethic, but prior to coming to the church, I took for granted the amount of control I had concerning how I used my time. I soon discovered that if I did not have some healthy, clear boundaries and take control of my schedule, then my time in the "tent of meeting" would be cannibalized by good, even important things.

God wants to meet with you. He wants to speak to you. Most

of the time He doesn't shout or scream at you, but He just wants your undivided attention.

Third, *when the people saw Moses going to meet with God, they were filled with anticipation.* Look again at verse 8: "Whenever Moses went out to the tent, all the people would rise up, and each would stand at his tent door, and watch Moses until he had gone into the tent."

The people came to expect something to happen because their leader met with God. Can't you imagine what was going through their minds? "I wonder what God is going to say to Moses today" or "I wonder what's going to be different because of Moses' meeting with God" or "What is God going to do for us after His meeting with Moses?"

God's people should be filled with a sense of confidence and expectancy when their leaders meet with God on a regular basis. When we meet with God, in essence we are pointing the people we lead to Him. Our habits model what really is core and important to us. When the people see the fruit of consistent communion with God in our lives, it gives them an appetite to do the same.

In fact, verse 10 tells us that when the people saw the pillar of cloud (representing the presence of God) at the entrance of the tent of meeting, the people would worship at their own tent door! This is compelling spiritual leadership. As leaders we must model what those whom we are influencing need to become and not just what we want them to do.

Are you aware how closely people are watching you?

Fourth, *Moses experienced a rare intimacy with God.* This is that "uncommon communion" that I mentioned in the last chapter. Fix your eyes on these holy, tender words in verse 11: "Thus the Lord used to speak to Moses face to face, as a man speaks to his friend."

Read those words again. Now sit back and close your eyes and ponder the implications of the awesome, holy, sovereign God of the universe speaking to a mortal, sinful human being as a man speaks to a friend.

This was a meeting of two friends who longed to see each other. And that's extraordinary, because it certainly was not a meeting of two equals. Moses was the one in need, but our great God in an act of love disclosed Himself to Moses. God did not become like Moses; He treated Moses like a friend because he honored Him. Psalm 25:14 says, "The friendship of the Lord is for those who fear him." The word "friendship" here could have been translated "secret council." Moses feared and reverenced God and because he did so, God moved toward his heart.

ADDICTED TO ACTIVITY

Earlier I mentioned some different occasions when I saw God lead me in an assignment even when I didn't know all the specifics. But I have also experienced the other side—the times when I did not consistently meet with God and wait on Him.

There's a certain "activity addiction" that is associated with leadership. Let's face it—as leaders we get a rush when we see things moving ahead and getting done. It's fun. And it should be! It encourages us to keep moving, to do even more.

But there is an inherent danger. We can get to the point where the stuff that we see accomplished can become in itself the reason why we do it. The action and activity becomes the call. And we drift away from listening to that sweet, assuring voice that says, "This is the way, walk in it." Sometimes we have an uneasy feeling about something and we somehow know that the Lord may be telling us not do something . . . or to wait.

Or we may take on more than what the Lord intended for us

to do. We don't listen. We don't do things the right way and we sometimes do the wrong things. We make assumptions about what He wants done. And like Moses, we find ourselves overwhelmed and worn out (Exodus 18:13–18). In our sincere desire to be faithful and to "get it all done," we sometimes misread our capacity and begin operating from a sense of guilt rather than a confident sense of God's direction that comes from the overflow of our communion with Him. We don't want to give up certain "good things" so we keep piling up stuff on what was once a pretty strong table. We place one more thing on the table and the weight is too much. The table crashes.

I have battled this tendency to "pile on" most if not all of my life. God continues to work on me in this area. By His grace and with the help of my dear wife and some close friends, I am getting better. But in 1987 I had a real scare. My inability to say no, and my inconsistency in spending time with God, left me worn out. I took some time off and God began speaking to me about my assumptions. Once again I saw my need to keep bringing everything to Him so that I might know His will and wisdom concerning what He wants me to do, what He wants me to not do any longer, and how He wants me to approach His assignments.

God never meant His assignments to destroy us but rather to call us to Himself. Once again, it's all about dependence. Leaders are not given the responsibility of telling their own story, or accomplishing their own dreams. God gives us His dream and unfolds His plan to us because He wants to do something special through us—and He wants to make us something special in the process.

Notes on Leadership

What is the relationship between the tasks/assignments God gives to you as a leader and your walk with Him?

Tim Kimmel

"If [a leader is] operating solo, he's going to find himself exhausting his options quickly. But when he operates in the power and presence of the God, with whom he is intimately engaged on a daily basis, he brings an infinite source of courage and endurance to the tasks/assignments before him. That doesn't mean he won't get weary or discouraged. But God's power and presence will surround him and empower him long after his human abilities have been exhausted."

Monty Watson

"We tend to think that our strengths are our strengths. Often, I realize that when I think I'm operating out of my giftedness and strengths, it's not really me. My strengths are really His strengths. I'm just not as talented or gifted as I think I am. He always does more of the heavy lifting."

Marvin Schuster

"My wisdom, my witness, my judgment is no better than my fellowship with Him, my obedience to Him and His Word."

Joe Stowell

"Being called to ministry puts all of us way beyond ourselves and leaves us with a healthy sense of insecurity and insufficient capacity to live up to the responsibilities. Which, in turn, thrusts us on Jesus to help us with the wisdom and discernment that we need to do His work. This required closeness to Him lets us experience Him in ways that make Him real to us and in turn real to our people. Any leader who does not find himself singing the old song, 'I need Thee, oh I need Thee . . . ' is in deep trouble. Self-sufficiency is the death stroke to authentic ministry and an open door to the devastating ramifications of pride."

Jim Reese

"If I look at my life and my walk with God, it is so clear looking back that my most effective times in business and in ministry are when I am close with God. Interesting when I think about it, it is a sweet time of communion with God at the tasks that need to be done. I think of these times especially when I saw no way to accomplish it but depended on Him and moved forward, learned, listened, and prayed heavily."

George Murray

"All tasks, great and small, need to be done in helpless dependence on the Lord, and not in the leader's own strength. Every major leadership task I have had has been bigger than my capabilities, causing me to cry out to the Lord who has revealed Himself by granting supernatural grace, strength, wisdom, patience, and courage."

Clyde Cook

"In order to maximize your effectiveness, you need to be close to Him. This has been so true in my life as I try to attempt great things for God, so if they are accomplished, people will say, 'There is no way Clyde could have done that. It must have been the power of God.' I am continually amazed at God's power, wisdom, grace, and love."

Ric Cannada

"The leader's walk with God is crucial. The more responsibility I have been given, the more I have felt the need for God's grace and wisdom and the more I have sought to carve out time to be alone with the Lord in the Word and prayer because I sense my need for guidance and the Lord's blessings on my efforts that are so feeble and shortsighted and ineffective in themselves."

SERVANTHOOD

AS AN IDENTITY

"Do nothing from rivalry or conceit, but in humility count others more significant than yourselves."

☀ PHILIPPIANS 2:3

"A man wrapped up in himself makes a small bundle."

☀ BEN FRANKLIN

AUTHENTIC
HUMILITY

My mother was a servant. She couldn't help herself. Serving was a part of her nature. Mom always
made sure that the people around her were comfortable and that they had their needs met.

She loved to help lift the burdens from people and
to make them feel special. She loved to share. As I was
growing up, we often had people sharing a meal with
us at our dinner table. Many times she would send me
to check on an elderly person in the neighborhood to
find out if they needed something or if there was
something we could do for them.

I remember once visiting Mom while she was in
the hospital. As I approached her hospital room, I
spotted my mother hobbling down the hallway with
her arms full of fruit. I asked her, "Mom, what are you

doing?" She explained that someone had given her a large basket of fruit. "Honey, there's some patients whom I thought would enjoy some of this fruit," she said. And then she enlisted me in helping to pass it out!

Mom would come down on my two sisters and me pretty hard if she felt that we were being selfish or we were mistreating someone. I remember her scolding me because I refused to give a certain family member a Christmas present. At the time I just didn't think that I should give this person a gift. I will never forget Mom cornering me, holding up her clinched fist, and saying, "When you hold your hand so tight around your life and the stuff that you have, God can't give you anything!" To this very day when I am faced with something that requires a bit of sacrifice, Mom's words come flashing across my mind.

Mom is with the Lord now. I can't begin to describe her influence, not only on me but also on so many others who knew her. It is powerful. She was a genuinely sweet, humble woman.

Too often we associate humility and service with being docile and weak, but I never thought of Mom that way. In fact, there was a dignity, a quiet strength, about Sylvia Loritts. She gave of herself and served, not because she was forced to, but because she wanted to. She was grateful to God for what He had done for her, and she believed that her calling was to be a source of blessing and encouragement to others.

I tell her story because her humility was attractive and because it was genuine. I think people were drawn to her because her giving was not based on getting something in return. And that is in stark contrast to the way I hear some people talk about "servant leadership."

STRATEGY? OR IDENTITY?

Nearly everybody who writes or speaks about leadership these days makes sure that somewhere in the discussion he drops in the phrase "servant leadership." To be sure, it's a necessary topic for Christian leaders, for it is the style of leadership Jesus modeled. And yet . . . I don't want to sound cynical, but some of what people mean about servant leadership is not the same thing as what the Bible teaches and distinctively Christian leaders model. Sometimes the expression is used in a utilitarian way. In other words, we need to be careful that we are not using servant leadership language as a strategy—as a means to manipulate people to do what we want them to do.

To be sure, as leaders we want the people whom we lead to be productive and effective in accomplishing the goal and the assignment. Certainly we want to create environments for them to be maximally effective. And when people are served, chances are they will be happy, motivated, and productive.

That is not the primary reason why we serve them, however. If it is, then we have fallen terribly short of what God's vision is for our leadership. Although we may be very effective at getting things done, over time the people we lead will see through our act. And they will see us as being disingenuous, loving and serving them as long as they do what we want.

So what is the answer? Where's the balance? I believe the key is *embracing servant leadership not as a strategy but as an identity.*

In other words, it's not something you do to bring about change or fulfill your agenda, but it is *who you are.* You are a servant just as much as you are a leader.

Joe Stowell puts it well when he says, "Don't think of yourself as a leader but rather as a follower of Jesus (Matthew 4:18; John 21:22). Most leaders have fallen because at some point of their lives they ceased to be a follower of Jesus and did it their way or succumbed to the seduction of Satan's way. Seeing yourself as a *leader* will tend to make you pushy and proud—two qualities that if practiced for long will make you a leader no more."

FROM HEAD TO . . . FEET

I will admit that it's not easy for a leader to be a servant; indeed, sometimes your responsibilities as a leader may, at times, seem to contradict the idea of servanthood. For example, being a leader means giving others a vision for the work God is calling them to do. As Bruce Fong says, "Vision gives the leader the responsibility to see the big picture and determine where a ministry is going. The leader then mobilizes the people to get the job done." My friend Jim Reese adds, "I think one of the greatest challenges for a leader is to move people to places that many times they don't want to go—but they are never the same once they have gone!"

I also should be clear that humility does not mean that a leader won't correct, give directives, rebuke, or, if necessary, terminate a person's employment. Genuine humility and servanthood does the right thing and is not self-serving. When the people we serve refuse to respond to what God wants done, then the decision has been made, and the best way of serving them is to move them on. It is not humility to refuse to do the difficult but right thing. It's much like my mother holding her clinched fist in my face and delivering a very clear message: "I will not tolerate selfishness from you because it is wrong!" Keep in mind that the same Jesus who washed the feet of the disciples (John 13:1–20) ran the hustlers and sellers out of the temple (Matthew 21:12–13).

I have been privileged to know some very influential Christian leaders who have been effective over time. One thing that impresses me about most of them is how little they talk about their leadership or the fact that they are leaders. They all know that they have been given a gift to lead. But they are defined by the privilege and opportunity to serve. They are able to lead and serve because their heart for God and passion to follow Jesus eclipses everything.

The core character quality out of which servant leadership flows is humility. There cannot be genuine servant leadership apart from genuine humility.

But what is humility? Does it mean to be passive? Does it imply a lack of confidence? Does it mean you should never acknowledge accomplishments and achievements? Does it mean that you should never allow your picture to be printed in a brochure . . . or on a book? (My picture is on the cover of one of my books, and someone told me that if I were truly humble, I would have never allowed that to happen!)

I realize that these and other related questions can border on being silly. Here's the point: Both pride and humility have, for the most part, very little to do with your actions and choices, but they have everything to do with your motives and attitudes. It is what you believe about yourself that determines whether you are proud or humble.

THE HUMBLE CHOICE

In a very real sense, humility is everything I have written about in this book. But let me try to say it more succinctly: *Humility is the intentional recognition that God is everything to you, and that you are nothing without Him. It is the acknowledgment that life is not about you, and that the needs of others are more important than your own.*

The humble person knows that humility is a *decision* (James

4:10; 1 Peter 5:5–7). As an act of the will he must intentionally anchor your choices and decisions to God and go about his business in such a way that exalts and honors Him. A humble person is concerned about what God is concerned about. A humble person is more God-conscious and others-conscious than self-conscious. At the end of the day the humble person wants to know that all he's done that day was done with the spotlight on the Savior.

Humility is also an *attitude*, a way of thinking that touches your approach to everything that you do and especially the people you come in contact with. Humility is the attitude and disposition that considers meeting the needs of others a joy and a privilege. That's the point of Philippians 2:3–11. Let me encourage you to absorb and meditate on these words:

> Do nothing from rivalry and conceit, but in humility count others more significant than yourselves. Let each of you look not only to his own interests, but also to the interests of others. Have this mind among yourselves, which is yours in Christ Jesus, who, though he was in the form of God, did not count equality with God a thing to be grasped, but made himself nothing, taking a form of a servant, being born in the likeness of men. And being found in human form, he humbled himself by becoming obedient to the point of death, even death on a cross. Therefore God has highly exalted him and bestowed on him the name that is above every name, so that at the name of Jesus every knee should bow, in heaven and on earth and under the earth, and every tongue confess that Jesus Christ is Lord, to the glory of God the Father.

Jesus humbled Himself in order to serve the purposes of God and to serve us. He is our example. We too must humble ourselves by serving the purposes of God and serving others. Just as Jesus sacrificed His life for our benefit (eternal salvation!), we too are called to sacrifice on behalf of others. True humility is a mindset, an attitude that causes us to give and to serve. It is evidenced by sacrificial service. Humility honors God by expressing His love and compassion through service to others.

CHECK YOUR DRIFT

When you serve, you send yourself a message: Stay humble. Russ Crosson, president of Ronald Blue & Company, observes, "The only way a Christian leader can stay at the pinnacle of Christian leadership is to serve, be humble, and never forget his roots." The greatest danger for a leader, Crosson says, "is to begin to read the press clippings and hear the applause and forget that it was God who put him there. I think in my case the greatest key to longevity is my wife, who keeps me humble and points out where the strength comes from. Really she would 'box my ears' if pride reared its ugly head."

Pride is always lurking in the shadows. You will never stop battling it. Here are a few questions you should ask yourself often to test whether you are drifting toward a proud attitude:

First, *are you teachable*? Are you gripped by a desire to learn more—not only about the Scriptures but about life? Do you listen to opposing views? Do you listen to those who report to you?

Jim Reese says, "One of the most important areas for all leaders, but especially young leaders, is the ability to continuously learn—learn from those around you, from the circumstances you are in, from the challenges and wins you have. Pride usually stops learning because the need to learn is many times not there. You can either feel you have arrived and thus don't need to learn, or because of your pride you are more concerned about how you look and sound than what you are doing or learning!"

In their book *The Leadership Secrets of Billy Graham*, Harold Myra and Marshall Shelley relate an interesting story told by Graham's youngest brother, Melvin. Billy was in the early stages of his ministry, but already had frequently preached overseas. Often when he visited Charlotte, North Carolina, he would spend time with a man named Bill Henderson, who ran a small grocery store in the African-American section of that town. "He was a tiny fella," recalled Melvin. He had long sleeves that came way down, and he wore a tie that would hang down below his waist. But I tell you, that little old man, he knew the Bible!"

Melvin said that Henderson "got beat up on many times, got his store robbed time and time again, but he just loved the Lord. I mean, he just *loved* God. Billy loved to hear Bill Henderson tell him about the Scriptures. He lived them; it wasn't weekend Christianity. And he could pray. He'd pray for Billy and his young ministry."

The book's authors loved the image of Billy Graham "taking time to sit on a crate to learn from a humble, authentic witness in the trenches." It's an example of a leader who has always been teachable.[4]

Second, *are you concerned with visibility and recognition, or with significance*? Many of God's greatest leaders are those who never receive the world's recognition for fulfilling His assignments. They go about their business faithfully, quietly, diligently, making tremendous impact that may not be evident through numbers and growth. I think of the pastor I had as a child, Burton Cathie, who led a church of about a hundred people. He worked other jobs because the congregation couldn't afford to pay him a full salary. Yet that man has marked me in more ways than I've realized. His life reminds me to never underestimate the significance and legacy of those quiet, steadfast leaders who are nurturing the faith of millions around the world.

Third, *are you overly focused on comparison and entitlement?* When you compare your ministry to those of others, you're either filled with a false sense of security because you're beating the "competition" (of course you would never use that word), or you become depressed because you are not doing as well as others. Either way it's become all about you.

Feelings of entitlement can ambush you at any time. You no longer feel humbled by the compliments and special treatment from others. You decide you deserve the recognition, the money, the perks. There's also a danger in spending too much time with other leaders. You lose touch with, in Russ Crosson's words, your "roots." You are drawn to the fraternity of "insiders" and if you're not careful, you become self-absorbed.

Steve Douglass is a real servant. In fact, those who know Steve will tell you that the thing that stands out about him is his heart to use the influence God has given him to bless and serve others. Whether it is in a meeting with international leaders or sitting down with a young new staff member who's trying to figure out how God has wired him, Steve is remarkably the same. He listens, and he looks for ways to help and to serve.

Serving for Steve is not a way to accomplish his agenda. He serves because he is authentically humble. So he doesn't adjust who he is by taking on a different demeanor so that he can impress the group that he happens to be with.

Because he travels extensively, Steve often receives first-class upgrades on his flights. But he regularly gives these upgrades to his assistant and takes a seat in coach. Steve doesn't do this so others will say, "Look how humble the president of Campus Crusade is!" And he doesn't encourage the other leaders in the organization to do the same. He does it to remind himself that leadership is a privilege—that his position should always be at the foot of the cross and not peering down from the top box on the organizational chart.

LEADING WITH POWER? OR PERMISSION?

The authority to lead is developed and cultivated not through prominence and power but rather through acts of service from a sincere humble heart. In this sense, others give us the "permission" to lead because they have experienced the authenticity of our acts of love and service on their behalf. This profound humility is God's way of leading His people.

"Serving is really the best posture from which to lead," Douglass says. "Not infrequently I am asked by leaders to 'grant them authority' to be in charge of something. They seem to want that trump card with those who report to them. A few days ago I had two of these conversations with two different young leaders. My advice in both cases was to love and serve the people who report to them and then they will have all the 'authority' they need to make their final decisions stick. By the way, both situations look like they are working out."

Bruce Fong observes, "Serving is the attitude and perspective that makes Christian leadership effective. Whether I am pursuing a potential donor, thanking a generous donor, or touching the life of a discouraged student, I am here to serve them with the gifts and resources that God has put at my disposal. I can't run this ministry alone. I value my faculty, staff, directors, students, donors, alumni, and local churches. As I serve, they too will serve and God alone gets the glory."

That's the message. People tend to follow who leaders are and what leaders do. We need to model not only the desirable behavior but also the desirable identity, a humble heart.

WHEN ROCKS ARE THROWN

God's pattern in Scripture is to use unlikely people to accomplish great things. We should never forget that the common denominator among all these great saints from the past is their humble commitment to God. As 1 Corinthians 1:26–31 tells us, God is glorified when we recognize we are nothing without Him:

> For consider your calling, brothers: not many of you were wise according to worldly standards, not many were powerful, not many were of noble birth. But God chose what is foolish in the world to shame the wise; God chose what is weak in the world to shame the strong; God chose what is low and despised in the world, even things that are not, to bring to nothing things that are, so that no human being might boast in the presence of God. He is the source of your life in Christ Jesus, whom God made our wisdom and our righteousness and sanctification and redemption. Therefore, as it is written, "Let the one who boasts, boast in the Lord."

Sometimes God has to send us a painful reminder that His assignments are not meant to be about us. I really don't like saying this, but through my own experience and studying and observing the lives of other leaders, I have come to conclude that often the only way to be reminded of authentic humility is to be humiliated. Failure and embarrassment dot the résumés of leaders.

This was King David's experience. His son Absalom was upset because he felt that his father did not do enough in dealing with an awful case of incest involving Amnon and his sister Tamar (2 Samuel 13). Absalom was handsome and winsome, but also a masterful deceiver. Over a four-year period he stole the hearts of the people from King David and overthrew his father (2 Samuel 15:1–12).

By the time David realized what happened, it was too late. He literally had to run for his life, taking with him a relatively small group of loyal followers, many of whom went all the way back to the days when he was on the run from another pursuer, King Saul.

Can you imagine how David felt? He was the most powerful king in the known world, a living legend, and now he was on the run. He was betrayed by his trusted friend Ahitophel (2 Samuel 15:12), and his own son wanted to kill him.

I've often wondered if perhaps part of David's problem was that he got a bit used to his position. Maybe he got a tad smug. Could it be that a little pride and entitlement caused him to lose touch?

But as David and his men were fleeing from Jerusalem, they had a telling encounter with a man named Shimei. As described in 2 Samuel 16:5–12, Shimei was obviously loyal to Absalom, and he cursed David and threw rocks at him. David's men were incensed and Abishai said to David, "Why should this dead dog curse my lord the king? Let me go over and take off his head."

Notice how David responded: If "the Lord has said to him, 'Curse David,' who then shall say, 'Why have you done so?' . . . Behold, my own son seeks my life; how much more now may this Benjaminite! Leave him alone, and let him curse, for the Lord has told him to. It may be that the Lord will look on the wrong done to me, and that the Lord will repay me with good for his cursing today."

This is nothing short of remarkable. David felt this experience was part of what the Lord wanted him to learn and experience. This is the epitome of humility. You don't curse a king and live! To David, it was as if God was telling him through Shimei,

"Face and embrace your humiliation and allow it to press the pride out of you and drive you to God."

I suppose you could argue that maybe David was simply distraught and didn't have the fire in his belly to deal with Shimei. Maybe he was depressed and irrational and he just wanted to quickly get to a safe and quiet place. But the story didn't end there.

When David's men put down the insurrection and he was reinstated as king, they ran into Shimei again. He had hitched his wagon to Absalom, had cursed the king, and now he pleaded for mercy (2 Samuel 19:16–20). Abishai reminded the king that he needed to take care of this unfinished business. It was not good for David's reputation to let this blatant disrespect and disloyalty to go unpunished. Abishai wanted to wipe the slate clean by wiping Shimei out (verse 21).

David did wipe the slate clean, but he didn't put Shimei to death. Instead he demonstrated that as king of Israel he was the humble servant of all the people, even those who cursed him. This was not a statement of weakness on David's part but a statement of enormous strength. Look at what this man after God's heart said (verses 22–23): "'What have I to do with you, you sons of Zeruiah, that you should this day be as an adversary to me? Shall anyone be put to death in Israel this day? For do I not know that I am this day king over Israel?' And the king said to Shimei, 'You shall not die.'"

Here's the point: David faced and embraced his humiliation, choosing to let it soften his heart. When he had the opportunity to use power, he used it to give someone what they did not deserve rather than to destroy a life to prove his "greatness."

Humility is the source of true greatness. It produces authentic servants.

"Jesus . . . laid aside his outer garments, and taking a towel, tied it around his waist. Then he poured water into a basin and began to wash the disciples' feet and to wipe them with the towel that was wrapped around him."

✳ JOHN 13:3–5

"People desire to be led but you earn the right to lead by doing the hard work of serving."

✳ JIM REESE

CHAPTER ELEVEN

THE DIGNITY
OF SERVING

When you think about it, the very word "servant" may cause you to picture someone who is controlled by someone else. Someone who has no freedom, no independence. It may not be a positive picture for you.

In fact, I have to tell you that, as an African-American, the words "servant" and "slave" are linked in my mind. Those words are reminders of that dark, painful period in the history of our country when my relatives were the property of white plantation owners. They were regarded as less than human and incapable of doing anything beyond menial tasks and serving the needs of those who controlled their lives.

So to me, there is not a whole lot of dignity associated with "servant"; just the opposite.

Even if you don't share my frame of reference, my guess is that you probably consider the role of "leader" to carry more dignity than that of "servant." Most of us have an unofficial criteria or "pecking order" to categorize people. That way we can determine who is more important, whom we want to emulate, and with whom we want to associate.

You know the game: We often tend to judge others' worth by the degrees they've earned, by the luster of their profession, or by the size of their home or bank account. And the people who serve us—those people who take our orders at restaurants, or make our beds in hotels, or fix the brakes on our cars . . . or those who report to us in our work—they are somehow less important, less worthy.

As leaders we need to be wary of the temptation to devalue people. It's pretty easy and seductive to think of ourselves as part of the "rare air" crowd. Because others don't have the recognition, education, and/or the accomplishments we may have, it's easy to conclude that we're the ones who deserve to be pampered and treated as special. Certainly leadership carries with it the weight of responsibility and additional accountability, but we are not special because we are leaders.

I love the way Randy Alcorn puts it:

I view leadership as a privilege, not an entitlement. Too many of us act as if we deserve a leadership role.

We've worked hard. So what? The guy at the tire shop works hard, the young mother works hard, the farmer works harder than we do.

We have skills. So what? The athlete has skills, but where do they come from? God. "What do you have that you did not receive? And if you did receive it, why do you boast as though you did not?" (1 Corinthians 4:7 NIV).

THE PROGRAM? OR THE PEOPLE?

Leadership as described in the Bible is not about glorifying those who are given the responsibility of guiding and directing other people. And it's not just about the assignments God gives us. *Leadership is also about the people through whom He wants to do His work.*

Joe Stowell says it is essential to see ourselves as "leading for the benefit of others." When we lead for the benefit of ourselves, he says, "those who are trying to follow us feel used and manipulated. Not a good thing!"

God never gives a leader a pass when it comes to loving and honoring the people around him or her. It is not a choice between getting the job done or treating the people with love, respect, and dignity. It's "all of the above."

Unfortunately, too many leaders love the tasks but just tolerate the people. They are real "getter-doners"—they place high priority on getting the job done. But to them, people are an expendable commodity. It's difficult for them to express appreciation or to communicate value to those they lead. They have little sense of their responsibility to serve the people they lead.

Jim Reese says the "biggest thing on my heart is the people the Christian leader is responsible for." He feels nobody should step into leadership without a willingness to assume responsibility for the people he leads. "I have seen so many wounded people by poor leaders who didn't take that responsibility seriously. I am sure we will stand before God and He will give us a report card on just how well we did this, how many times did we do it out of selfish ambition rather than a heart for God and for our people."

And how do you think people feel about working under these leaders? They have no sense that their work is appreciated, no awareness that they are being served, and no idea of how their contributions fit into the greater picture of what God wants to accomplish through them.

One of the convictions I have developed through the years is that those who work with me or report to me should feel as if I have invested more in them than I have asked them to give. I want them to be better people because they've hung around Crawford Loritts. Even if they profoundly disagree with me, I never want them to feel as if I did not love them or care about who they are as people.

Admittedly, this has not always been easy to do, especially when I have had to make a tough decision that collides with the position someone on my staff takes. Or when someone is not performing well in his job. But even in these circumstances—even when you need to let someone go—it's possible to let people know you value them and care about them.

THE DIGNITY OF GOD'S IMAGE

Our natural tendency to judge and classify people leads us to make some wrong conclusions about the word "dignity." Dignity is not something that you acquire or arrive at after years of outstanding accomplishment and achievement. You are not dignified because of your family name or reputation, or because of you are well known to others. It's not something you earn by becoming a doctor, a lawyer, or a successful businessperson.

Dignity is tied to the nature of being human. Dignity is the enormous weight and value that every person is born with because we are created in the image of God. *Dignity is God's signature written on the soul of every human being.* It's as if God says, "Every person has weight and value because they bear My image."

And my point is simple and hopefully clear: We have no right to minimize or marginalize the value of any human being. Honestly, some of us treat our pets with more dignity than we do certain people.

Each of us is born with innate dignity because we are created in the image of God. And we are called to live lives that reflect the nobility of that identity. Our attitude toward every person should not devalue the image of God that is stamped on their souls. Every person is entitled to hold his or her head high and walk with certain, confident steps because the God of the universe has created him or her in His image.

Dignity is an important word when we talk about servant leadership. Dignity gives nobility to serving. The responsibility of every leader is to be obedient to the call and at the same time enhance the dignity of those who work with him. *It is your job as a leader to cause those around you to feel their worth and value as those made in the image of God.*

Jim Reese is a very successful business executive and he happens to be one of the most respected leaders at our church. I have had the privilege of working very closely with Jim. One of the things that I am most impressed about him is his ability to stay focused on a task and in the process develop the people working on the task. He communicates value and treats them with dignity. He is quick to call, e-mail, or send handwritten personal notes— all to let you know that he cares about you.

People absolutely love working with Jim because they know he loves the people around him. When you work with him, you feel special. You know that he wants to get the job done, but you also know that he wants you to be better in every way because of the experience. Jim does this because he primarily views himself as a servant.

Jim doesn't lead from power but from the posture of a servant. As a result he not only maintains the dignity of the people around him, but he also enhances it.

By the way, it is dangerous to give someone a position before he is ready for it. Too much prominence and power is too great a temptation for many! I have seen more than a few people who were given positions of leadership that were beyond their ability to handle. Invariably, they began using their position to control others because they were afraid that their weaknesses and failures would be discovered. A lot of damage is done when the "position" becomes the identity and not the platform to advance the mission and to enhance the dignity of those who come in contact with them.

HOW DID JESUS LEAD?

As followers of Christ, we should always consider Him as our model, our example in all things. So it is with leadership. I can summarize the essence of biblical leadership in one sentence, six words: *It is to lead like Jesus.*

How did Jesus lead? How did He relate to those who followed Him, particularly His disciples? What can we learn?

It is both simple and yet profound. Jesus led by serving. And He served because He was and is a servant. He demonstrated that there is great dignity in being a servant leader.

I want to draw your attention to two moving passages in which we see the heart and passion of Jesus, the great Servant Leader. The first is Matthew 20:20–28. Look closely at these words:

> Then the mother of the sons of Zebedee came up to him with her sons, and kneeling before him she asked him for something. And he said to her, "What do you want?" She said to him, "Say that these two sons of mine are to sit, one at your right hand and one at your left, in your kingdom." Jesus answered, "You do not know what you are asking. Are you able to drink the cup that I

am to drink?" They said to him, "We are able." He said to them, "You will drink my cup, but to sit at my right hand and at my left is not mine to grant, but it is for those for whom it has been prepared by my Father." And when the ten heard it, they were indignant at the two brothers. But Jesus called them to him and said, "You know that the rulers of the Gentiles lord it over them, and their great ones exercise authority over them. It shall not be so among you. *But whoever would be great among you must be your servant, and whoever would be first among you must be your slave, even as the Son of Man came not to be served but to serve, and to give his life as a ransom for many.*"

Notice how Jesus turned this request—from a mother who wanted her sons to get the recognition that she felt they deserved—into a lesson about God-honoring leadership. The ten other disciples were upset at what they considered brazen audacity, and began politicking and positioning themselves for prime spots in the kingdom. Jesus used this opportunity to define true greatness.

He did this by contrasting the approach and motivation of the "rulers of the Gentiles" (verse 25) with what should be the motivation of His followers. The "greatness" of the Gentile rulers was based on two things. The first was *position*—the Gentiles "lord it over them" (verse 25). They were above the people and they let those under them know exactly where their place was. They took every opportunity to remind their subordinates that they should stay in their place.

Similarly, the "greatness" of these Gentile rulers was based on *power*. Look at the expression "exercise authority over them" (verse 25). They were quick to use the power they had. If you didn't do what you were told, or you didn't do what was expected, there was a price to be paid. The primary leadership tool was intimidation and fear. My way or the highway!

I know a man who held a position of leadership in an organization, and he constantly talked about his position and his authority to fire people. He just had to let you know how important he was. If you crossed him, you'd pay for it. On more than a few occasions, he proved his point by giving subordinates their walking papers.

He was a frightened, insecure man who should have never been given any position of leadership. Why? Because he had not yet become a servant. He may have gone through the motions of servanthood at times to make it appear that he was a servant leader, but he had not embraced it as an identity. Remember, serving is what servants do as part of their nature.

This is what Jesus defined as greatness. You must *be* a servant. You don't just act like a servant; you must become one. You are only ready to lead when you stop trying to prove your worth and value based upon your position and power.

You are loved and embraced by your awesome God, and you cannot make Him love you any more than He does. And because you are profoundly loved and valued by Him, you are free to be a channel of love and blessing to others. You are free to serve.

LEADING WITH A BASIN

This brings us to a second extraordinary passage of Scripture, John 13:1–13. This is the passage where Jesus washed the disciples' feet.

Jesus was about to be crucified. The disciples had spent a little more than three years with Him. They had been through it all —miracles, confrontations with religious leaders, powerful pronouncements, and riveting messages from the Lord. Now the crowds were gone and they were together alone with Him in this house eating supper.

On this occasion, only days before He would die on the cross for their sins, Jesus did something that would not only mark the disciples for the rest of their lives, but would also be a signature of authentic Christianity and Christian leadership in particular. It was nothing short of astonishing: Jesus rose, took off His outer garments, tied a towel around His waist, poured water into a basin, and washed the disciples' feet.

Stop and think about how these disciples felt. The Creator of the universe, the everlasting Son of God, was on His knees washing their feet. This was a holy moment. Undoubtedly there were tears running down the cheeks and beards of these rough but ordinary men. Silence. The only sound was the water dripping off the feet in the basin.

Dignity. Value. That was the message. Jesus was saying by this act of service, "I love you and I want you to forever know that I affirm all that God made you to be. I am your servant."

But there is more. He did this as an example. Soak in John 13:14–15: "If I then, your Lord and Teacher, have washed your feet, you also ought to wash one another's feet. For I have given you an example, that you should do just as I have done to you."

As a leader, you must never forget that you belong to the community of the towel and the basin. Your authority to lead is directly related to your ability to serve. When you have washed feet, the people you lead will know that you value them.

SO THEY'LL "WANT TO KNOW MORE ABOUT HIS JESUS"

During the 2008 Olympic Games in Beijing, it was interesting to note a number of new articles in the press about Eric

Liddell, a former missionary in China who is held in high esteem in that country long after his death in 1943. You may know about Liddell from the Oscar-winning movie *Chariots of Fire*, which told about the challenges he faced reconciling his Christian faith and his superior ability as a sprinter approaching the 1924 Olympics. Perhaps the more amazing story about Eric Liddell, however, is what occurred after he captured the 400-meter gold medal that year.

Liddell, who was born in China to Scottish parents serving as missionaries, returned to the land of his birth as a missionary in 1925. To read about his ministry there is to read about a man who was convinced of the assignment God gave him and was committed to leading by serving.

Many of the most dramatic stories focus on his final years in north China, when the area was the center of conflict between China and Japan. In 1939, for example, Liddel joined Dr. Kenneth McAll at the London Mission Hospital in Siaochang, which was in the center of the war zone. "As Britishers we were not popular with the Japanese, who suspected us of spying," McAll writes, "and as Christians we were unpopular with the Communists who only tolerated our presence because they could use our hospital for their wounded. However, it was always possible to get caught in the crossfire. On several occasions he and I, when cycling across open fields to visit sick or needy people in another village, would have the sudden thought to get off our bikes and take cover, only to hear bullets flying over our heads. God's guidance was very real to both of us."

On one occasion, Eric heard of a man who had survived a Japanese ambush and attempted execution, and had been lying at the scene for ten days. He and a nurse loaded him on a cart and brought him to the hospital, where he recovered over a period of weeks. "One day he called out to me in English," McAll writes. "He said he was so interested in what he had heard from Eric and others, and was so impressed by the care he had witnessed, that he wanted to know more about his Jesus they talked about."

In 1941, British nationals were advised to leave the country. Liddell's wife and children moved to Canada, but he stayed on to continue serving the people he loved. Then, in 1943 he and other nationals were interned at a Japanese camp in Weishien, and he continued his ministry there—teaching science and directing sports for the camp school, teaching Sunday school, school, helping families in need, helping resolve conflicts. "He was everywhere, he was ubiquitous," recalls the Rev. Dr. Norman Cliff. "One moment he was speaking to us schoolboys in his cheerful way, then he was gone and he'd be seen talking with some businessmen half a mile away. Wherever he went, he brought confidence and happiness."[5]

Liddell died of a brain tumor a few months before the camp was liberated, but he led and served with such dignity that his impact is still felt today.

His life reminds us that we should lead not from power and position but as a messenger sent to deliver value and dignity. Are there times in which you need to use the authority of your position? Yes, but never for self-serving motives.

In fact, if you know who you are, not only are you secure enough to serve but your authority becomes obvious. The less power you use, the more you have.

It is those who serve others who are kingdom leaders.

Wash feet!

Notes on Leadership

What have you learned about serving while leading?

Monty Watson

"A Christian leader is much like the conductor of an orchestra [who] plays none of the instruments. Yet the conductor is responsible for getting the best out of each musician, leveraging each person's gifts (playing the right instrument), getting all the musicians to play together in symphony. By not playing any of the instruments, the conductor is free to serve the members of the orchestra. He can hear wrong notes, he can know when they are not playing together. The conductor-leader is available to others and free to say, 'How can I help you?'"

Tim Kimmel

"What I've learned is that serving and leading are synonyms."

Dwight McKissick

"A servant attitude and actions are of paramount importance with regard to gaining the confidence of others; who will then allow you to serve and lead them."

Joe Stowell

"Jesus told His disciples that they were to be 'servants of all.' I've had the opportunity to understand that the time of refreshing for me is often when I'm serving others. In the natural, it may seem like not the best use of a leader's time, but in kingdom work, we always need to be close to the heart of ministry, which is helping people understand who God is, and in loving our neighbor as ourselves."

Jim Reese

"I believe all great sustaining leaders serve. I don't think you lead long term without serving. You might be able to walk in their shoes but truthfully many times you can't or won't because it is not what you do but serving them by listening, answering questions, giving them time, translates in the same way!"

Michael Little

"People are fragile and can't be taken for granted if the leader desires greater unity and productivity from the team."

Robert Lewis

"The more you can model in real life serving and honoring others, the more power you have as a leader."

Sheila Bailey

"[Those we lead] must witness us serving them and others so they will learn how to walk in our footsteps as we follow Christ."

Dolphus Weary

"Those I lead follow in a greater way when they know that I am demonstrating a servant heart."

"For I am already being poured out as a drink offering, and the time of my departure has come. I have fought the good fight, I have finished the race, I have kept the faith."

✳ 2 TIMOTHY 4:6–7

"We must not cry 'Go on,' but 'Come on.' Our people may justly expect of us that we should be among the most self-denying, the most laborious, and the most earnest in the church, and somewhat more."

✳ CHARLES SPURGEON

CHAPTER TWELVE

THE POWER

OF SACRIFICE

During the months that I've been writing this book, I've noticed a television commercial that portrays a boss talking with several of his male employees in a video conference. Unfortunately for them, a backdrop behind them collapses, revealing that they are not sitting in an office but at . . . a golf course!

In their failed attempt to fool their boss, these men also reveal their fanatical devotion to golf. To them, work is just a necessary part of their lives that enables them to pursue their real passion.

In a similar way, I think your approach to leadership can reveal whether it is a passion or just a diversion. If you have been called to lead, then leadership to you is not a hobby. It is a *calling*. You have a stewardship responsibility before God to be diligent and faithful wherever He has placed you. The assignment, whatever it may be, must be accomplished.

But here's the key: If you are passionate about being a leader, you must not only be deeply, passionately committed to God and His assignments for you, but you also must be committed to the people through whom He wants to accomplish His work. And there's one sure way to test that commitment—one way to prove whether leadership is a hobby or a passion: *Are you willing to sacrifice yourself in order to serve those who serve you?*

"LOVE WITH CLOTHES ON"

The other evening Karen and I saw a movie about a high school basketball phenom. It was a moving story of a young man who had overcome incredible opposition and challenges. His mom raised him and his younger siblings by herself in a dangerous inner-city neighborhood.

His father was nowhere to be found . . . until he showed up when the son was drafted by an NBA team! Now he wanted a relationship, but the young man asked, "Where were you when I needed you?" He went on to tell his father that the person he could count on and who sacrificed for him was his mother. Her sacrificial love for her son knitted their hearts and lives together.

At the heart of biblical leadership is a bond and a love for the people who share the call and assignment. The question every leader needs to ask is, "What am I willing to do so that the people I lead know that I love and care for them?" The answer is *sacrifice.* Just as the mother in this account demonstrated her love by sacrificing for her son, a leader will need to show his love and commitment by sacrificing his own needs and desires in order to serve them.

A wonderful sense of community is formed when we are committed to a common purpose. We love and care for each other in a special way because we share a common mission, cause, and values. This draws us together and can create a synergy based on mutual commitment and sacrifice that will cause the group to be better than any one individual could ever be. The model to this community of sacrificial love is the leader.

I love how Chip Ingram, my friend and an author and Bible teacher, describes sacrifice. He says, "Sacrifice is love with clothes on." Being a servant leader means not operating from power or position but laying aside your rights and picking up a towel and bowl of water to wash feet.

The leaders who have marked my life most deeply have been those who demonstrated that they were willing to sacrifice to help me grow and mature. I think of Dr. Douglas MacCorkle, former president of Philadelphia Biblical University, who believed in me and, out of his own pocket, paid for promotional materials that launched my ministry. Then there's Olan Hendrix, the former general director of the American Missionary Fellowship and my first boss in ministry, who used his name and support to open doors for a young, inexperienced twenty-two-year-old preacher. I can remember a number of occasions when Bill Bright, founder of Campus Crusade for Christ, adjusted his schedule so that he could support a project or event to which I was giving leadership. He would go out of his way to help. His door was always open to me.

STAMPED ON SCRIPTURE'S PAGES

Sacrifice is the evidence of your commitment to God's call and to the people you serve. Sacrifice is the window through which others clearly see your heart for them and your desire that they not fall short of anything God wants them to be or to do.

Sacrifice says you are willing to do whatever it takes to make that happen.

Sacrifice also is an expression of your faith and confidence in God. You can give to others because you know that God will take care of you. And out of gratitude for God's great sacrifice in giving His Son so that you would be set free from the death sentence of sin, you give to others.

This sacrificial attitude is stamped all over the pages of Scripture. Abraham gives up his right to have the best land so that Lot can be happy. Nehemiah leaves comfort and security and risks everything so he can fulfill God's call to rebuild the hopes and the lives of his people back in Jerusalem. Ruth lays aside her future so that she can love and care for her mother-in-law. Esther puts her life on the line to save the Jews. Jonathan risks his life and rejection by his father, Saul, in order to help his friend David fulfill God's call for his life. The list is endless.

Contrary to every instinct and intuition in you, the way to profound fulfillment and an overwhelming sense of purpose is to give yourself for others. It is in dying to yourself for the right reasons that you find yourself and experience life to the fullest. This was Jesus' point in John 12:24–25 when He said, "Truly, truly, I say to you, unless a grain of wheat falls into the earth and dies, it remains alone; but if it dies, it bears much fruit. Whoever loves his life loses it, and whoever hates his life in this world will keep it for eternal life." Grain will never produce wheat unless it is planted in the ground. It has to be buried in order to produce any good.

Too many of us are spending too much time and energy on ourselves. Our spiritual crop is limited—and even nonexistent—because we refuse to be buried. We're standing on top of the soil, insisting, "Hey, look at me, and watch where you're stepping. Don't you know that I'm a unique, special piece of grain?" Our self-absorption is hurting our ability to love and give to others so that they can soar and be all that God intended for them to be.

In fact, we are unwittingly engaged in a sort of *negative* discipleship, teaching others by our example that we should help and give to others only up to the point when we have to sacrifice ourselves. Is it any wonder that we increasingly speak of the responsibilities placed in our hands as a job or career and not as a sacred trust worthy of our call? I fear we are witnessing the erosion of the nobility of sacrifice.

THE WARDROBE OF SACRIFICE

A servant leader will be called to sacrifice himself in many different ways. Here are a few:

1. Dealing with difficult people. I'm sure you've heard the old line "Leadership would be great if it weren't for the people!" Just think what we could accomplish if we didn't have to deal with motivating apathetic people, answering innumerable questions, and working through their differences and disagreements with us. I will admit that through the years I've worked with a number of people who caused my heart to race and my defenses to switch on to full alert each time I saw them. I would think, "Here comes trouble!" and wish I could hide in my office.

In my case, it seems as if God makes sure that I always have somebody like this around. Why? Because He wants me to love and give even to those who irritate me. He reminds me that part of His assignment involves helping people like this grow in their faith. And He reminds me of the times I've been difficult to people I reported to!

2. Giving up the urge to "just get the task done." I often need to remind myself that completing the task may be only a small part of an assignment from God. For those of us who are driven by a need to work and to complete a job, this is a very hard balance to hold in tension. We are haunted by the pressure to get the job done.

And it's easy to see those who report to us as mere instruments to help complete the task. Oh, how it stings when someone says, "I only think you care about me when you want something from me or when you want me to work a little harder." Especially because I know what it feels like to be the object of someone's "relational strategy" to help them accomplish their agenda. I know a few guys who only seem to call me when they need or want something. You should hear the conversation; you would think we hung out together on a regular basis.

3. Investing in those who report to you. Sometimes this requires a sacrifice of your *time*. For example, you may be facing a huge workload and you feel the pressure to devote all your time to completing it, but you also see the need to spend time training someone in how to do their job. Or you need to spend time outside the office with your coworkers to develop a better relationship.

Investing in others also may require a sacrifice in your *prominence*. You love preaching on Sunday mornings, but you give up speaking slots to an assistant pastor who needs the experience. You prefer to give presentations yourself, but you assign some to a subordinate to help him develop his skills. Some of you may even be very aware that you are training your replacements—that at some point a subordinate will take your place, and you may even end up reporting to him! This is assuming the attitude of John the Baptist, who knew that as Jesus began His public min-

CRAWFORD LORITTS 163

istry, his own would end: "He must increase, but I must decrease" (John 3:30).

4. Giving up time with family. While there are many who lose their families in their drive for success, there are others who swing to the other extreme. While we don't want to be workaholics and lose our families while we are fulfilling God's assignments, some have made family an idol. They have neglected and, in some cases, abdicated God's call for their lives because they wrongly assumed that this was an either/or proposition—they refused to let anything come in the way of family commitments.

In fact, God may want to use the sacrifices associated with your calling to build and strengthen your family. For example, the nature of what I've been called to do means that I've had to travel and be away from my family. I can't tell you the number of times I wrestled with feelings of guilt because I missed a child's ball game, recital, or some other event. I was torn because I love my children, and didn't want them to grow up feeling that I neglected them. I didn't want them to despise what I did because it took me away from them. But as Karen and I discussed it, we developed the conviction that there were times when I needed to follow God's call on my life even if it meant I couldn't always be there for my family.

Our four children are adults now and they, too, are involved in ministry. Our two sons are both preachers, doing pretty much what I've done for most of my life. I marvel and scratch my head in wonder at the goodness and grace of God to Karen and me. We placed our children in God's hands and often prayed this prayer: "God, because You have called me to this ministry, please give me wisdom and show me how to be a good husband and father. Please take care of them in every way as I give myself to what You have called me to do." I know it sounds simple, but God answered this prayer.

In no way am I suggesting that we should neglect our families. We certainly need to give them what they need and deserve in terms of our time and attention. And one of the most important lessons in life is that sometimes there must be justifiable sacrifices. There are times when they should lay aside what they would like or want for no other reason than it is the right thing to do.

PAUL AND TIMOTHY

I am drawn to the moving passage of 2 Timothy 4:6–8. Here the great apostle Paul encouraged the young leader Timothy to give himself completely to the calling and to the people God has given to him.

As I read the entire letter of 2 Timothy, I am impressed with the depth of love and commitment Paul had for Timothy. In fact, Timothy was like a son to him. In 2 Timothy 3:10 Paul praised Timothy for following his example: "You, however, have followed my teaching, my conduct, my aim in life, my faith, my patience, my love, my steadfastness . . . " In short, the message is, "You're doing great. I'm proud of you."

Paul wrote Timothy from prison and was about to be executed for proclaiming the gospel. But his parting words for his son in the faith were not a call for sympathy but a challenge to embrace and emulate the sacrifices made on his behalf by his mentor. Let these words grab and encourage your heart:

> *For I am already being poured out as a drink offering*, and the time
> of my departure has come. I have fought the good fight, I have
> finished the race, I have kept the faith. Henceforth there is laid

up for me the crown of righteousness, which the Lord, the righteous judge, will award to me on that Day, and not only to me but also to all who have loved his appearing.

✳ 2 TIMOTHY 4:6–8

Notice the expression "poured out as a drink offering." Paul borrowed this word picture from the story of King David's mighty men who risked their lives by breaking through enemy territory just to bring back water to David from his favorite well in Bethlehem (1 Chronicles 11:17–19). When David realized that they had put their lives on the line to provide him with this luxury, he was overwhelmed and refused to drink the water. Instead he poured the water out on the ground as an act of worship and thanksgiving to God for the love and sacrifice of these men for him.

By using this expression, Paul said his life is like the water that David poured out on the ground before the Lord. Paul wanted Timothy to know that he was joyously giving his all for Him. It was a part of God's call. It was an act of worship.

Who are you pouring your life out for? Do the people you serve know and feel that they are a priority to you? Are you giving more to them than you are taking from them? Do they see your leadership flowing out of the integrity of your love and commitment to them?

Do you wear the wardrobe of sacrifice?

RADICAL, IMMEDIATE OBEDIENCE

"But I do not account my life of any value nor as precious to myself, if only I may finish my course and the ministry that I received from the Lord Jesus, to testify to the gospel of the grace of God."

✳ Acts 20:24

"Sustaining oneself in ministry requires a group of friends. No one can go it alone. That group of friends must be honest, confidential, have fun, and go deep."

✳ Monty Watson

STAYING IN
THE GAME

Through the years I have talked to many older, veteran Christian leaders. Many of these conversations have been nothing short of a worship experience because they are so focused on their Lord and Savior.

I love listening to their stories. Often I ask, "What motivated you to do what you've done?" Sometimes they tell me about events that have been "strangely" orchestrated in their lives and served to point them in a certain direction. Or they will share how they were gripped by a need or burden that something needed to be done and they felt compelled to act. But almost to a person, they say that they did what they did because they *had* to. It was a matter of obedience to God. They would rather die than disobey God.

Obedience. The very word says it all. Biblical leadership is characterized not only by brokenness, uncommon communion, and servanthood but also by *radical, immediate obedience.*

There is no such thing as leadership apart from action. But to the Christian leader it is not just action that matters, it is *obedient* action. There is a big difference between chasing good ideas and fulfilling a mission, an assignment. I've said it many times already in this book, but please let it grab you: God is about the business of doing through us what He wants done. Leadership is the stewardship process by and through which God's assignments are implemented. To be a leader is a sacred trust. Our faithfulness in doing what God says is what really matters.

BETTER THAN THE FAT OF RAMS

Some years ago we had some extensive renovations done in our basement. It turned out to be a bit of a nightmare because the contractors simply were not faithful to do what we asked them to do and they had agreed to do. We went back and forth with them. Finally, although still not completely what we wanted, we could "live with" what they did and we were happy to see them move on.

Experiences like this remind me of that dreadfully sobering encounter that Samuel, the priest, had with King Saul. God had told Saul through Samuel that he and his people were to destroy the Amalekites, including their livestock. Well, Saul did defeat the Amalekites, but he spared the life of their king, Agag, and allowed his people to keep the best of the livestock. As 1 Samuel 15:19–23 describes, God revealed this to Samuel, and Samuel confronted Saul.

"Why then did you not obey the voice of the Lord?" Samuel asked. "Why did you pounce on the spoil and do what was evil in the sight of the Lord?"

Saul protested that he had obeyed God. "I have gone on the mission on which the Lord sent me. I have brought Agag the king of Amalek, and I have devoted the Amalekites to destruction. But the people took of the spoil, sheep and oxen, the best of the things devoted to destruction, to sacrifice to the Lord your God in Gilgal."

All of us leaders should have Samuel's next words permanently chiseled in our hearts and minds: "Has the Lord as great delight in burnt offerings and sacrifices, as in obeying the voice of the Lord? Behold, to obey is better than sacrifice, and to listen than the fat of rams. For rebellion is as the sin of divination, and presumption is as iniquity and idolatry."

Notice that obedience is more important than our religious ceremony and acts of worship ("sacrifice"). Disobedience is called "rebellion" and likened to witchcraft ("divination"). When God is specific and clear about what He wants you to do, He does not give you the option to freelance or to improvise. Such "presumption" is called "iniquity" and "idolatry." Think about that: Whenever you choose your way over His way, you commit idolatry because, in essence, you are saying that your wisdom is superior to God's. You are acting as though you are God.

Let me press into this a bit further. You could argue that Saul *generally* did what God told him to do; he destroyed most of the Amalekites and some of the livestock. Okay, he doesn't get an A, but isn't he at least good for a B– or C+?

To God, however, this was not good enough. When God speaks, obedience is not something to be negotiated. There's no such thing as partial obedience. We either completely do what God says or we disobey Him. God is to be taken seriously.

I wonder how much more could be and would be accomplished for the glory of God if we listened to God and did everything He told us to do? I sometimes think about those times in my life when I didn't completely do everything God told me to do. What more would God have done—how more people would have heard the gospel, or how many would have been mobilized for the cause of Christ? Maybe you think about these things too. I am so grateful for God's forgiveness and grace. He really is the God of the "second chance" and the third and the fiftieth! The consequences and lessons we learn from our disobedience should humble us and make us more responsive to God and passionate about obedience.

That's one of the reasons why I am pleading with you (and myself!) to please take this matter of obedience seriously. If you have been operating out of a reservoir of "good ideas" and have not led with seeking God first, listening to Him and then taking steps of obedience, let me encourage you to repent and to get your priorities in order.

HEALTHY AUTHORITY

Obedience acknowledges the supremacy of God over all things, including the affairs of your life and the work/mission He has called you to accomplish. You are His. What you do is His.

Your attitude toward obedience is often influenced by your attitude toward authority. On numerous occasions I've observed a mother at a grocery store trying to control a child who is completely out of control. Little Johnny is running wild, pulling items off the shelves, or he's pitching a fit because she won't buy him some cookies.

Now, one of two sequences usually occurs. In one scenario, Mom's anger bursts out and she treats Johnny roughly—jerking him around, calling him cruel names, perhaps using obscenities. In the other, Johnny doesn't listen to Mom, and she keeps threatening him, but she doesn't follow through. She promises Johnny that he's going to "get it." But instead Mom is the one who is "getting it"—a royal work over by her sweet little boy.

In either instance, I walk away feeling really bad for that kid. Johnny is learning some bad lessons about authority. Either he's learning not to take authority seriously, because he gets what he wants with his manipulative behavior, or he's learning that authority is selfish and unjust, and he shouldn't trust it.

Sadly, many people carry these attitudes about authority into their lives as adults. Some have been deeply hurt by parents who abused or neglected them, withholding the love and attention they desperately needed. Others trusted leaders who betrayed them or manipulated their emotions. Some placed too much confidence in a church or an organization only to be profoundly disappointed.

But here's the problem: We tend to project our negative experiences with authority onto God. We either have problems trusting God, or we develop our own theology, making Him a "softer God" who demands very little of us.

God loves you with an infinite, unimaginable love. God is nothing like an abusive, neglectful earthly parent. God is not a needy, insecure, power-hungry leader. You cannot compare Him to an imperfect, inconsistent organization or church. Your concept of God should not emerge from the painful bitter experiences of this life. You dare not let your view of Him be contaminated with the sinful inconsistencies and imperfections of His fallen creation and creatures. Your concept of God and the nature of His authority should be derived from what He says about Himself in His Word and not from your experiences or your speculations about who and what He should be like.

God is to be trusted and to be completely obeyed. He is our Creator and the ultimate authority.

CONTENT? OR COMPLACENT?

Our lives were meant to be the story of God in human history. God is making His statement through us. Certainly He has given all of us different personalities, talents, gifts, and experiences. As His followers He demands that we give everything back to Him so that He can leverage all that we are to accomplish what we were born to do (Romans 12:1–2; Ephesians 2:10; Proverbs 3:5–6). It is our destiny.

As a leader you can become comfortable and settle in to a routine and rather predictable life. You begin to like the way things are, and you lose the sense of destiny I just described. The processes are working. The challenges are manageable. You begin to think that what you've done in the past and what you are doing now is what God *always* wants you to do.

It is one thing to be content; it's quite another to be complacent. It becomes easy to ignore the promptings of the Spirit of God to embrace God's next assignment. We rationalize and settle into a comfortable disobedience. Gradually our fruit diminishes, our impact wanes, and we are left wondering, "What happened . . . What's missing?"

I would like to suggest that when you struggle with knowing your destiny, and with finding meaning and purpose, these feelings may be the manifestation of disobedience. When God speaks to you and you choose not to obey Him fully, or even ignore what He is saying, He will allow you to experience frustration, emptiness, and despair.

But that's only one result of not walking in obedience to God. Returning to the story I began earlier about King Saul, it is sobering to see what God does after Saul's disobedience. This led God to say, "I regret that I have made Saul king, for he has turned back from following me and has not performed my commandments"

(1 Samuel 15:11). As the apostle Paul writes in Acts 13:22, God removed Saul and "raised up David to be their king, of whom he testified and said, 'I have found in David the son of Jesse a man after my heart, who will do all my will.'"

Obviously David and Saul were very different. David had cultivated a tender, responsive heart toward God ("a man after my heart"). At the end of the day David wanted more than anything else to please God and to honor Him.

This story shows me that you can never get too big or too important for God to replace you. God is not impressed with your past accomplishments or your stature—especially because He gave you that stature in the first place. When you refuse to obey Him, He will find someone else who will. He will simply turn around and say, "Next!"

It is an unspeakable privilege and opportunity to be entrusted with assignments and responsibilities given to us by the Ancient of Days. But it is not a good thing not to do what He says.

DISHES OF PURE GOLD

This doesn't mean that David never failed. In fact, we know that he failed miserably; he committed adultery and murder (2 Samuel 11–12). His behavior was inexcusable and God made sure that he paid the consequences. But unlike Saul, who lied when he was confronted by Samuel about his sin and disobedience (1 Samuel 15:13–14), David said only six words when Nathan the prophet confronted him: "I have sinned against the Lord" (2 Samuel 12:13).

David was crushed by the guilt of his sin and the conviction of the Holy Spirit. So much so that he wrote Psalm 51, the song of his deep remorse and repentance concerning his sin. Look at what he says in Psalm 51:1–4:

Have mercy on me, O God, according to your steadfast love; according to your abundant mercy blot out my transgressions. Wash me thoroughly from my iniquity, and cleanse me from my sin! For I know my transgressions, and my sin is ever before me. Against you, you only, have I sinned and done what is evil in your sight, so that you may be justified in your words and blameless in your judgment.

David was called a man after God's heart because he responded to Him . . . even after he sinned! This gives all of us hope. God is looking for leaders who are not perfect but who respond to Him; leaders who don't make excuses about their sin or justify patterns of disobedience; leaders whose hearts are tender and responsive to the conviction and correction of the Holy Spirit.

I think of a comment by Clyde Cook: "I want to be used for God's highest purpose. I have another card on my desk with 2 Timothy 2:20–21 from the Living Bible: *If you stay away from sin, you will be like one of those dishes made of purest gold—the very best in the house—so that Christ Himself can use you for His highest purposes.* Obviously if our Lord Jesus Christ has a highest purpose, it must mean that He has some lower purposes. I want to be used for His highest purpose. The secret of this, of course, is in the first part of the verse, 'if we stay away from sin.'"

Saul was afraid of losing his position as the leader of Israel. But David was afraid of losing the touch, intimacy, and favor of God who had been everything to him. Honestly, what are you more afraid of?

FIT INTO GOD'S PLANS

I am intrigued by the idea of being a man after God's heart, like King David. Second Chronicles 16:9 says, "For the eyes of the Lord run to and fro throughout the whole earth, to give strong support to those whose heart is blameless toward him." He is looking for men and women who will obey Him, and when He finds them, He gives them greater and greater assignments.

There is a story of a young woman who pleaded with God to show her how He wished to use her life. She considered becoming a missionary in China or Japan, but did not feel God was leading her there. She also wished to marry and start a family. And this led to an important crossroads, when she fell in love with a handsome young banker in her small town. In many ways he seemed a perfect match for her, but she was troubled by the difference in their spiritual lives.

The young man attempted to win her over. A friend of hers later wrote,

He tried to make her see that he admired her religious convictions; he tried to persuade her that they could establish their home and she could go on and believe and do just as she wanted and she wouldn't have to change in any way . . . Yet she could not get away from this thought: it would be like establishing a home and deciding that the husband would eat in the dining room and she would eat in the parlor each night. They would both have a good meal, but they would not be dining in fellowship. If in the matter of faith they could not sit at the same table and have fellowship together, their relationship would be impossible. It was the time of her greatest decision . . . and she prayed in solitude: "Lord, You have made me the way I am. I love a home, I love security, I love children, and I love him. Yet I feel that marriage under these conditions would draw me away from You. I surrender Lord, even this, and I leave it in Your hands. Lead me, Lord, and strengthen me. You have promised to fulfill all my needs. I trust in You." She knew that she would leave at the end of the year and terminate their friendship.[6]

God blessed the faith of this young woman, and began to use her in significant ways as a leader in her church, influencing young people for Christ. Eventually she realized that she had been called "to train leaders and to nurture the spiritual growth in thousands who could go in her place to penetrate the world with the Gospel of Christ."[7] Her work caught the eye of a pastor of a large church in Southern California, and he hired her as the Christian education director.

This woman, Henrietta Mears, stayed in that post at Hollywood Presbyterian Church for the next thirty-five years, until her death in 1963. During those decades God used this single woman in such a powerful way that she can safely be called one of the most influential Christian leaders of the twentieth century. Her ministry of discipleship was so dynamic that she played a significant role in the lives of young leaders such as Billy Graham, Bill Bright, and a multitude of other individuals who went on to help change the world.

Henrietta Mears was totally committed to her Savior, and she demonstrated this commitment through her obedience. Her heart was His. And though she once worried about what she would miss if she didn't marry and have children of her own, she later commented, "The marvelous thing has been, as I look back through the years, that the Lord has always given me a beautiful home; He has given me thousands of children; the Lord has supplied everything in my life and I've never felt lonely."[8]

WHEN IT'S TIME TO LOOK BACK

Have you ever noticed that there is a sweet, godly nobility about certain older leaders? I never knew Henrietta Mears, but in many leaders I have known, I've noticed a joy and a calm assurance and a strength that emanates from their demeanor. God has honored and rewarded their obedience. They carry with them a wholesome fear of God because they have seen Him honor their faithful response to what He placed before them to do. This should be our vision and passion too.

My dear friend Tim Kimmel puts it this way: "The guys who seem to last the longest and maintain a fresh passion for their calling are the ones who walk hand in hand through the highs, lows, and mediocre moments of their ministry. They take their cues from God and gain their strength from Him. One of the litmus tests I look for is the level of joy they have in their work even after they've been at the same assignment for twenty or thirty years. This is no great secret. It's exactly what God said would happen if we make Him the primary focus of our life."

God's faithfulness should inspire our complete, immediate obedience.

Notes on Leadership

What gives longevity and "staying power" to leaders?

Steve Douglass

"Love for God, love for people, learning to like what you have to do."

Joe Stowell

"Living life in front of people in a way that consistently reflects the love and integrity of Jesus . . . a life worthy of respect . . . a life that reflects the authentic power of true humility that gives substance to what you preach."

Steve Farrar

"We are to count various trials as joy . . . These sufferings are what produce endurance that enable us to finish strong. We must also be ruthless to keep ourselves in the Word of God. We must read it, chew on it, ponder it, and apply it with more vigor as we grow older. I also think that we must be afraid of ourselves and our potential to commit great sin. We must keep a close watch over our lives. We are called to live by a higher standard."

Sheila Bailey

"Consistent prayer, focusing on God's faithfulness in my life and the lives of others, focusing on Scriptures on perseverance and commitment, journaling my prayer requests and how God answered my prayers, listening to the testimonies of others, being transparent, seeking wise counsel, dialoging with a mentor."

Ric Cannada

"Longevity and 'staying power' comes from personal time with the Lord; a supportive, loving wife; and at least a few close friends who care and support and encourage you."

Monty Watson

"Sustaining oneself in ministry requires a group of friends. No one can go it alone. That group of friends must be honest, confidential, have fun, and go deep."

Marvin Schuster

"Keeping my priorities in order (God-family-work-to include prayer and study and meditation on Scripture). Trusting much in the Lord and very little in yourself. Proverbs 3:5–6. Work as unto the Lord."

Dwight McKissick

"Integrity, effectiveness, and the wisdom to understand and relate to the time and people without compromising biblical principles."

George Murray

"Paying attention to all three 'gauges on the dashboard' of your life: the physical gauge (proper sleep, exercise, diet), the spiritual gauge (the Word, prayer, fellowship, and accountability), and the emotional gauge (margin, downtime, Sabbath-keeping). Also, a supportive, godly spouse and close friends."

Bruce Fong

"Longevity is connected to good mentors. I could have humanly quit on many occasions. One mentor in particular urged me to shoot for longevity. Each leader should gather a good collection of mentors who are older and experienced to have free access into our lives."

Jim Reese

"I think it is exciting to see what God is doing, to wake up with an excitement and anticipation of that. These don't need to be only big things, in fact, if we lose sight of the 'little things' that God does we lose so much joy. I also think you have to guard yourself in getting trapped in doing ministry rather than serving God. I think when we are serving God our focus is not on us but what He is doing—we celebrate what He is doing."

"They all wanted to frighten us, thinking, 'Their hands will drop from the work, and it will not be done.' But now, O God, strengthen my hands."

✳ NEHEMIAH 6:9

"Understand that God will sustain you. The enemy wants quitters, the culture hates strong Christians in leadership, but He calls us to endure."

✳ MICHAEL LITTLE

ENDURING

THE CHALLENGE

When I was in eighth grade, my parents were not pleased with the grade I got in science. They thought I was capable of doing better, so after the school year they sent me to summer school; if I could earn a higher grade, it would replace the original.

To say the least, I wasn't happy and I did not want to go. I'm not proud of this, but I sort of wore my mother down with my bad attitude and protests about being in summer school. When I figured I had ma-nipulated my mother to the point that she would give in, I announced to my teacher after class one day that I wouldn't be back.

Then he said something to me that struck deeply. It was one of those powerful, direction-altering state-ments that would serve as an anchor in my life for years to come. He looked me in the eye and calmly but clearly said to me, "Crawford, if you quit now, you probably will be quitting for the rest of your life."

Those words stopped me in my tracks. I suppose one of the reasons is because my dad wasn't a quitter. Although summer school was not as big a deal to Pop as it was to my mother, I could hear echoing from the teacher's statement what my father said so often to me, "Boy, finish what you start!"

I can't count the times through the years that those words from that science teacher come roaring back to mind. You see, he was calling me not only to work hard but also to be courageous—to set aside my attitude, to not accept mediocrity, to persevere through the hardship.

SEE IT THROUGH

When Karen and I went through two years of intense adversity and trials during the early years of our marriage and I seriously thought about leaving the ministry we were a part of, I remembered those words. It was as if God spoke to my heart and said, "See it through."

During seasons of attack and criticism, I often hear those words and once again God says to my heart, "See it through." When my shoulders slump under the load of pressure, disappointment, and discouragement, I will retreat to a quiet place to pour out my heart to God. And yes, those words visit me and again God will say to my heart, "See it through."

I share this because in recent years I have been spending more of my time with younger leaders. My life has been enriched by so many of these young men. Their vision, passion, and energy are contagious. I am high on this next generation and I believe the cause of Christ is in good hands.

But there is one issue that keeps cropping up in our conversations. It is the issue of courage. Many of these rising leaders grapple with fear. At times this struggle leads to an inability to take courageous action in implementing the assignment God has given to them.

To be sure, fear has been with us since the beginning of time. And it is safe to say that all of us are afraid from time to time. It's also safe to say it's not a good thing to follow leaders who claim to have never struggled with fear. They have two glaring problems: They are not truthful, and they have a distorted self-perception!

But I think that the dismantling of our families over the past fifty years or so has almost institutionalized fear and uncertainty. Divorce, the rise of single-parent households, and the tragic assortment of abuse and dysfunction in our families have produced a generation with many young people who are afraid of risk, and afraid to make mistakes.

So many of our young men grew up in homes in which they had limited or no contact with their fathers, or they had dads who were detached and didn't provide any meaningful leadership. We are left with a legacy of men who in varying degrees have been feminized. They are uncertain about who and what a man is, and how a man acts and behaves. They are fearful of assuming responsibility and taking the initiative in charting direction.

My heart aches for the young men who have gifts and abilities but are afraid to lead. They seem to have everything that they need, but they shrink back—they won't see it through. Perhaps they have been so beaten down by failure and disappointment in their past that their confidence is gone. I'm sure this is a big part of it. But I also believe that having a dad or a father figure in their lives—someone who modeled manhood, imprinted their lives, and made them do what they didn't want to do but so desperately needed to do—would have given them the "courage under fire" to see it through. I am tired of the devil paralyzing these young men with fear and robbing the church of the vision, passion, and sanctified ideas that they could bring to the table.

Would you join me in praying that God will continue to raise up older godly mentors who will come alongside these young men and pour into them God's love, confidence, and encouragement? So many did it for us; now it's our turn.

MOSES SEES IT THROUGH

I've heard a number of definitions of courage over the years, but I like to think of it as *complete obedience in the face of opposition.* That opposition comes in many forms: hardship, personal struggles, weaknesses, attacks by the devil, and outright hostility from people who attack what you are doing.

The story of Joshua in the Old Testament is a lesson in courage. Joshua was a young man whom Moses had mentored. And it was one amazing course in leadership development! For forty years Joshua walked and lived in the shadows of Moses, the great deliverer and lawgiver. In an earlier chapter I mentioned that Joshua did not want to leave the Tent of Meeting (Exodus 33:11) because he was overwhelmed by the presence of God and, no doubt, inspired by Moses' passion for God's presence. Joshua learned so much about leadership from Moses, not the least of which was the necessity of obedience and courage.

Joshua was an eyewitness to the miracles and also to the challenges to Moses' leadership. He watched his mentor press into the calling and the assignments God placed before him. He saw Moses persevere through opposition, failure, and discouragement. He saw the greatness of God brilliantly on display against the backdrop of a mere man who was committed to radical, immediate obedience. Joshua also saw Moses develop and thus knew that obedience carries a price—profound self-denial. As I said in the last chapter, God's leaders don't do what they want to do—they are men and women who are under His authority and they follow His direction.

But there was one failure, one act of disobedience that prevented Moses from experiencing the fulfillment of the vision.

The book of Numbers describes how the Israelites grumbled and complained despite God's continual provision for all their needs. Even though God had miraculously freed them from slavery under the Egyptians, by the time they reached the edge of the Promised Land, they refused to believe that God could give them victory over the people who lived there (Numbers 13–14). By the time we reach Numbers 20, the Israelites are still grumbling about their leadership, namely, Moses and Aaron. The trigger this time was their need for water.

Like an infection, negative disbelief spread throughout the camp. They insulted God and their leadership by saying it would be better if they were back in Egypt, the place of oppression and death.

Moses turned to God and asked what he should do. And God told Moses to "*tell* the rock before their eyes to yield its water" (Numbers 20:8). But Moses was angry. He was sick and tired of enduring the toddler tantrums and challenges of these people. So instead of "telling" the rock to yield water, he took his staff and hit the rock twice. Water gushed out (20:12), but look at what happened next:

And the Lord said to Moses and Aaron, "Because you did not believe in me, to uphold me as holy in the eyes of the people of Israel, therefore you shall not bring this assembly into the land that I have given them."

At first glance, you might be tempted to conclude that God was severe, too harsh. But remember that God had disclosed Himself to Moses in a way that He had not done to any other man. Exodus 33:11 says, "Thus the Lord used to speak to Moses face to face, as a man speaks to his friend."

With great disclosure comes great responsibility and accountability. Further, notice God's remark that Moses failed "to uphold me as holy in the eyes of the people of Israel." Moses' failure to do exactly what God said was an affront to His holiness. The people had gotten to Moses and out of frustration and anger he responded the way they had. He did not model obedience. And it cost him dearly.

As a leader God calls you to model obedient action instead of reflecting the unbelief and negative attitudes and behaviors of the people whom you lead. Apart from the power of the Holy Spirit, this is impossible to do. But you must embrace and press into this kind of obedience. People can and will get under your skin if you let them. You need to remember that anger and cynicism will eventually cause you to unravel and will disqualify you for leadership.

A DRAMATIC ENCOUNTER

Joshua witnessed all these events. No doubt the consequences of his mentor's disobedience would later fuel his courage to see it through. It is a good thing to remember the failures of those we admire. It reminds us that we are capable of doing the same thing and it causes us to depend on Him and to trust Him for the strength to do it His way.

Just before Moses died, he brought Joshua up before the Israelites. In front of the nation he commissioned Joshua as their next leader (Deuteronomy 31:7–8). Then Moses died.

I wonder what Joshua was thinking? Flashing through his

mind must have been a vivid montage of those God-moments with his mentor—life lessons and encounters he experienced with Moses. In his mind's eye he could see Moses lifting the staff and the Red Sea parting. Ringing in his ears was the voice of Moses saying, "Thus says the Lord!"

But I can imagine something else that Joshua must have been feeling. He had been chosen to lead in the place of Moses. He was responsible for governing the people and leading them into the Land of Promise. The shadow of Moses was over him, and a daunting, unfinished task lay before him. To be sure, fear, uncertainty, apprehension, and inadequacy struck his heart. He needed courage.

In one of the most moving, dramatic encounters in the Bible, God personally came to Joshua and spoke directly to him. Think about it! God Himself addressed this leader, and in so doing He poured confidence and courage into Joshua's soul.

God's inaugural message to Joshua is found in Joshua 1:1–9. This is the finest descriptive definition on courage you will find anywhere in the Scriptures. Whenever you are feeling rattled and threatened by fear, find a quiet place and bury yourself in this passage. You will find the strength and courage to obey God despite your fears.

I find myself reading this passage often. In fact it was the text for the first message I preached at the church I pastor.

THE INAUGURAL SPEECH

It's interesting to observe how God began. He started by saying to Joshua, "Moses my servant is dead" (1:2). I see two important implications in this statement. First, no matter how great Moses was—and he was a great man of God—he was mortal. It's wonderful to admire the faithfulness and accomplishments of others. We should be inspired by their lives, especially their obedience. But they are flesh and blood, and like all of us they die.

Second, this statement was a reminder to Joshua that Moses died but the assignment was still very much alive. God grabbed Joshua's attention. The message was: there is work to be done!

There's an old line that says that when a man of God dies, nothing of God dies. God's work is passed on from one leader to the next until the task is completed. The death of a leader does not affect what God wants to accomplish. This should appropriately humble us and help us to keep our part in what God does through us in perspective. This frees us from developing a "messiah complex," assuming that we are indispensable to God and to the people who depend on us.

When you die, God will raise up someone else to replace you. And that person may even do a better job!

Now that God had Joshua's attention, He proceeded to speak about courage. God cuts right to the heart of Joshua's fear and uncertainty. I want to highlight four descriptive elements of courage that I see in this monologue.

THE CHARGE: BE COURAGEOUS

First, *courage rests on a clear assignment from God* (Joshua 1:2–4). In very clear terms, God repeated the assignment that He had originally given to Moses and is now Joshua's job description: "Arise, go over this Jordan, you and all this people, into the land that I am giving to them, to the people of Israel" (1:2). God was telling Joshua that he is to be courageous *for* something.

It is foolish to talk about courage apart from something that needs to be done. The task/assignment gives context to courage. Again, we are courageous *for* something. Courage is only required when we are charged to do something in the face of opposition or threat. No matter what is thrown at us, we have to do what God has clearly charged us to do.

Second, *courage rests on the assurance of God's presence.* God never calls you to do anything without also assuring you of His presence. To do what God says means to carry His presence and resources with you. I love what God said to Joshua in verses 5 and 9: "Just as I was with Moses, so I will be with you. I will never leave you or forsake you. . . . For the Lord your God is with you wherever you go."

When I was a little boy I was afraid of the dark. I would love it when my dad would stay in the room until I fell asleep. I thought my dad was the bravest man in the world. I knew he had it all under control. Nothing could or would bother me as long as I knew that Pop was nearby.

God doesn't tell you to do something and then leave you to fend for yourself. You are operating under His authority and for His glory. The mission is His and you are His. He will protect you, provide for you, and give you the resources to see it through. Can you imagine the sense of comfort and confidence that must have come over Joshua when God told him that just as He had been with Moses, He would be with him? Flash back to the Red Sea, the Tent of Meeting, the glory of God shining on Moses' face when he descended from Sinai. And now God would be with Joshua in the same way?

If you are doing what God has called you to do, He is with you. You are not alone. I know, sometimes you feel as if you are. Even as I write this chapter, I'm also thinking about a few difficult decisions I have to make. I need to apply what I am writing about. Earlier today I felt a sense of loneliness, as if I was all alone facing these things by myself. But that's a lie. God is with me and He will give me what I need to do that is required. Praise His name!

Third, *courage rests on focused determination.* Notice that, in Joshua 1:6–9, three times God commanded Joshua to be courageous: "Be strong and courageous . . . Only be strong and very

courageous . . . Have I not commanded you? Be strong and courageous." Courage is like a muscle; it grows stronger with use. When
you act with courage, and move forward in obedience, your faith
and resolve to persevere is strengthened.

Perhaps you are low on courage because you stopped moving
ahead. Like a muscle that has atrophied, your courage has grown
limp and lifeless. The answer is to get off of the couch and stop
making excuses for your lack of progress and mediocrity. Get back
in the game, and start obeying God. You'll be stronger and you
will feel better.

Of course, there is another reason why God commanded Joshua
to be courageous. He was about to face real, heavy opposition as he
led the Israelites into the Promised Land. The people living there
were not going to open a welcome center with a banner across the
front, saying, "Welcome Israel! We're Delighted That You've Come
to Take Our Land!" No, there was going to be a fight.

Anytime God gives an assignment, you can expect opposition. The world, the flesh, and the devil are in league to force you
off track and to defeat what God wants done. It's one thing to
hear God speak to you; it's quite another to actually do what He
says while you're being attacked. And the fiercest assault is always
directed at the leader.

Leadership is not about the conference room or the board-
room; it is all about the battlefield. Leadership is always about
verbs, action. It is not about the safety of ideas (as important as
that might be), but about implementation and movement in the
face of opposition. And that takes courage.

I love what Michael Little says: "Understand that God will
sustain you. The enemy wants quitters, the culture hates strong
Christians in leadership, but He calls us to endure."

Fourth, *courage rests on knowledge of and obedience to the Word of God.* Look closely at Joshua 1:8, "This Book of the Law shall not depart from your mouth, but you shall meditate on it day and night, so that you may be careful to do according to all that is written in it. For then you will make your way prosperous, and then you will have good success."

THE RESPONSE

The key to his life and leadership, God told Joshua, was to do everything that He said in His Word. Joshua was is to *proclaim it* to the people ("not depart from your mouth"), he was to *possess it* ("meditate on it day and night"), and he was to *practice it* ("be careful to do all that is written in it").

Success or failure is determined by your obedience to the Word of God. You are offered the same choice as Joshua. You can either try to sustain yourself by your talent and experience, by positive self-talk and motivational slogans, or by the strength of your strategic plans. Or you build your life and ministry on the Word of God.

Your courage to live and to act is tied to God's promises found in His Word. When you make your plans in line with His Word, and allow His Word to truly be the final authority for how you live, you can be assured of His blessing. If you want to be a godly leader, you must determine to both lead with the Scriptures and to live according to the Scriptures.

Courage is found in a clear assignment from God, the assurance of God's presence, focused determination, and the Word of God. In the words of Tim Kimmel, "Being a leader in God's cause is not only an honor, it's a sacred trust. We come under higher scrutiny. It's not for sissies. But to them who receive the call and report for duty with a humble heart, it is the greatest job in the world."

"Therefore, since we are surrounded by so great a cloud of witnesses, let us also lay aside every weight, and sin which clings so closely, and let us run with endurance the race that is set before us."

＊ HEBREWS 12:1

"In my life, typically God has used difficult circumstances, times, and disagreeable people to help me understand, often in hindsight, what He has prepared for me in ministry."

＊ KEN BEHR

CHAPTER FIFTEEN

THE LEGACY OF FAITHFULNESS

The other day, I was talking with a good friend who has an international radio ministry and is an author and speaker. He has been at it for many years now and is an influential leader with a ministry touching millions of people's lives.

We were talking about God's faithfulness in our lives. In the middle of our conversation, he began to chuckle. I asked him what was so funny. He said he marvels at what God has done through his life. He pointed out that he is not particularly smart or unusually gifted. But he believes that what has made the difference is that by God's grace he has pursued faithfulness. That resonated deeply in my heart.

Over time, faithfulness wins hands down. There's no comparison. It's not even close. It's good to be smart, gifted, and faithful. What a wonderful combination! But intelligence and ability will only get you so far. Faithfulness will carry you across the finish line.

A faithful person is one who steadily follows God and obeys Him consistently. Faithfulness is the stuff of stability, the evidence of purpose, the signature of commitment. Faithfulness demonstrates that we take responsibility and accountability seriously. Faithfulness says that we believe that God's assignments are important.

As I write these words I see the faces of gifted leaders I have met through the years, full of promise and ability. Sadly, some of them never realized the potential wrapped up in their dreams and ability. They took shortcuts. They coasted. Because they were quick studies with attractive personalities and persuasive public gifts, they did what they liked to do, what they wanted to do, but not very much of what they should have been doing.

I think of a young, promising leader I met some years back who, despite his obvious abilities, had very little discipline. Initially he was like a pied piper—people were drawn to his charismatic personality and his ability to speak. He had a quick mind, and with very little effort he could put presentations together and captivate his audiences. The problem was that "very little effort" became a habit. He became increasingly lazy. He wouldn't complete his assignments.

Several of us pointed this character flaw out to him. To date he hasn't changed. But what has changed is the response of the people. His laziness has done damage to even his natural abilities. He's not quite as sharp, and others have taken note. You would not call this young man faithful.

If you desire to serve God long term . . . if you want your life to count . . . if you want to leave a legacy with your children and with the people you serve as a leader . . . you will pursue faithfulness in your life.

FAITHFULNESS IS GRATITUDE IN MOTION

During a recent trip to Chicago, I took a taxi. The driver was from a country in Africa; he and his family moved to the United States a few years ago. As we talked I discovered that he had two jobs and worked long hours. But he wasn't complaining. In fact, I could hear the joy in his voice as he described his gratefulness for the opportunities he and his family had in this country. He worked hard because he was grateful.

As leaders, we should be profoundly grateful that the God of the universe would give us gifts to use, call us to lead, and entrust us with His assignments for our moment in history. We should not treat what God has placed in our hands as an entitlement or a means to impress others. No, everything we have is a treasure from God to be used for His glory. He made us His child and commissioned us to serve Him while we have breath. And our response should be to "get after it" with all that is in us. Why? Because we are grateful for the privilege to express our love and gratitude for all that He has done for us!

The apostle Paul connects faithfulness and gratitude in two key New Testament passages. Look first at 2 Corinthians 4:1, 6, which tells us:

> Therefore, having this ministry by the mercy of God, we do not lose heart . . . For God, who said, "Let light shine out of darkness," has shone in our hearts to give the light of the knowledge of the glory of God in the face of Jesus Christ.

Paul was grateful for the grace of God, and for the knowledge of Him; as a result, he did not "lose heart"—he was faithful. And in Philippians 3:12–14 we find these words:

> Not that I have already obtained this or am already perfect, but I press on to make it my own, because Christ Jesus has made me his own. Brothers, I do not consider that I have made it my own. But one thing I do: forgetting what lies behind and straining forward to what lies ahead, I press on toward the goal for the prize of the upward call of God in Christ Jesus.

Christ made Paul "His own," and in gratitude Paul continued pressing forward to fulfill what God called him to do with his life.

Christ has made you His own. So don't give up—keep pressing. Why? Out of gratefulness for what God has done for you.

FAITHFULNESS IS RESPONSIBILITY IN MOTION

A friend once told me that his father never used an alarm clock. Before he retired, his dad always got up before dawn to go to work. One day out of curiosity my friend asked his dad why he never needed an alarm, and the father's response was priceless: "Responsibility woke me up every morning!" He had a mortgage to pay, mouths to feed, and a future to secure. Responsibility told laziness, "Take your hands off of him. It's time for him to get up and get after it!" His dad took seriously his assignment to care and provide or his family. He owned that responsibility.

Throughout this book leadership has been presented not as a hobby or a point of interest but as a sacred trust. As a leader, you have been called to do something, to accomplish something for the honor and glory of God. It is in your daily choices that you demonstrate how seriously you take that responsibility. It is what you decide to do when the daily alarm clock of responsibility goes off that makes the difference. Will you shut it off and roll over and go back to sleep? Or will you get up and greet it with gratitude and holy ambition?

Randy Alcorn captures this point when he says, "A long obedience in the same direction is, to borrow a Eugene Peterson phrase, sustained by the small choices we make each day. We need to be acutely aware of the cumulative nature of our little choices. What I eat and whether I exercise will determine the state of my body. Whether I read Scripture and great books or watch TV and listen to talk radio will make me into the person I will be five years from now. I should discipline myself today, not for discipline's sake, but for the purpose of godliness" (1 Timothy 4:7–8).

The key expression is "the cumulative nature of our little choices." The young man I mentioned earlier apparently underestimated the synergy of all the little decisions he made each day. Choices and decisions become patterns and habits; they become exponential in their force and impact. If they are the wrong decisions, or even not the best decisions, over time our faithfulness is damaged. We are left with dreams and desires but no discernable footprints in the sands of time.

On the other hand, good choices over time demonstrate faithfulness, and God rewards that faithfulness with increasing responsibility. "When we obey God in the small things, he will give us an opportunity to hear His calling for ministry," says Ken Behr, former president of the Evangelical Council for Financial Accountability. "I've found that God's revelation is in proportion to only what we have been proven faithful and therefore are prepared to accept."

As leaders we are faithful stewards of what belongs to Him.

That means He tells us what to do with what He has entrusted to us. I love the way Paul puts it in 1 Corinthians 4:1–2: "This is how one should regard us, as servants of Christ and stewards of the mysteries of God. Moreover, it is required of stewards that they be found trustworthy."

I should also mention that a leader's responsibilities often include a lot of stuff you don't want to do, but that stuff comes with the territory. God's assignments are not always about making you happy. As I wrote earlier in this book, hardship and difficulties are part of the leader's portfolio, his calling. You prove yourself to be faithful and trustworthy by weathering the storms.

In fact, one thing I've learned to look for when I am recruiting or interviewing people for leadership positions is what I call the "show-up" factor. I want to hear about experiences that were hard and difficult, and how they handled their responsibilities. This is an insight into the degree of their faithfulness.

FAITHFULNESS IS A SINGLE MIND IN MOTION

Distraction is the archenemy of the leader. Good, wonderful things can distract you from that one "God-thing" you have been called to do. Most leaders in varying degrees wage war with the lure of good things and compelling ideas and ventures that divert them from being faithful to their primary calling. You get sold and sucked in only to regret it later on.

There are three things I have learned to do when I'm presented with a tempting opportunity. First, I ask God to show me if this is something I should do or be involved in. Second, I say to myself, "Just because I *can* do this doesn't mean that I *should* do it." Third, I will seek the insight and wisdom from those close to me.

Here's what I have learned: Distractions can cause you to be faithful about the wrong stuff! Our hearts are right but we just got pulled slightly off course. Things are not exactly right and our primary calling is spinning its wheels. We can't seem to get traction.

In the early 1990s I was, among other things, giving leadership to one of the national ministries of Campus Crusade for Christ, maintaining a very busy speaking schedule, and sitting on several boards of organizations. That was all in addition to my responsibilities as a husband and father. I was tired, and I began to question my effectiveness. A dear friend said to me one day, "There comes a time when you have to stop doing the things that you can do, and even the things that you are improving in, and *concentrate on the things you were born to do.*" God used those words to get me to focus.

What are you born to do? Are you faithfully focused on doing that? Let Paul's advice to the young leader Timothy calibrate your decisions and activities:

And what you have heard from me in the presence of many witnesses entrust to faithful men who will be able to teach others also. Share in suffering as a good soldier of Christ Jesus. No soldier gets entangled in civilian pursuits, since his aim is to please the one who enlisted him. An athlete is not crowned unless he competes according to the rules. It is the hard-working farmer who ought to have the first share of the crops. Think over what I say, for the Lord will give you understanding in everything.
✳ 2 TIMOTHY 2:2–7

Paul was underscoring to Timothy the relationship between focus and faithfulness. Once again, he was telling him to not let anything get him off track.

We need to ask the hard questions about our schedules and workloads. We are not all the same—what may be considered as a distraction to one person may very well be a focus to another. And there are times when focus means different things at different times. But in each season it's important to seek God's wisdom about whether you are focused enough on God's assignments for your life.

FAITHFULNESS IS GRAVITAS IN MOTION

Gravitas is a Latin word, the root of the English words grave and gravity. *Gravitas* means to have weight and substance. Often it refers to those who bring a sense of moral focus, weight, and substance to their moment in history.

God's leaders who are faithful can't help but bring a sense of holy *gravitas* to their environment. "Walk in a manner worthy of the Lord" (Colossians 1:10). When we do God's will, our lives are characterized by a worthy "walk." Our faithful obedience to His will, as I said in the last chapter, ensures that God's unique presence will be with us.

Daniel was faithful. He was God's man and his life was marked by *gravitas*. He was not defined by his times, but in a wonderful sense his life brought definition to his times. The unbelieving, godless Babylonian Empire did not touch him, but instead he touched it for God. *Gravitas*. Because he was faithful to God, God protected Daniel and honored him and granted him favor and stature.

But this all began when Daniel was a young man and made a decision that marked the course of his life. He decided that he would not defile himself by eating the king's food, which probably included meat that had been offered to idols (Daniel 1:8). Though the decision would be tested three times (Daniel 3, 5, 6), he passed each time, as he did not flinch when it came to faithfulness to God. And God did not flinch when it came to honoring His faithful servant.

WHEN THE CALL IS ANSWERED

Another person who brought a sense of gravitas to his moment in history was William Wilberforce, the heroic English moral reformer. In many ways, the story of Wilberforce is the story of a man who lived out the qualities of a Christian leader that I've described in this book.

God gave Wilberforce an incredible, seemingly impossible assignment for his life. As Wilberforce wrote in his diary in 1787, a year after he converted to Christianity, that God had called him to work for "the suppression of the slave trade."[9] As a member of Parliament, and with many influential friends, he realized God had put him in a position to make a difference as a public servant. "My walk ... is a public one," he said, "my business is in the world; and I must mix in assemblies of men, or quit the post which Providence seems to have assigned me."[10]

It is difficult to imagine the difficulty, the seeming impossibility, of the assignment God gave to Wilberforce. Today we consider slavery to be a terrible evil, but as Eric Metaxas writes, "In the world into which Wilberforce was born, the opposite was true. Slavery was as accepted as birth and marriage and death, was so woven into the tapestry of human history that you could barely see its threads, much less pull them out."[11]

The slave trade was a vital part of Great Britain's foreign income. To oppose it not only meant confronting powerful economic forces, but also trying to change the minds of people who did not believe slavery was immoral. As Metaxas writes:

> *The opposition that he and his small band faced was incomparable to anything we can think of in modern affairs. It was certainly unprecedented that anyone should endeavor, as if by their own strength and a bit of leverage, to tip over something about as large and sub-*

stantial and deeply rooted as a mountain range. From where we stand today—and because of Wilberforce—the end of slavery seems inevitable, and it's impossible for us not to take it largely for granted. But that's the wild miracle of his achievement—that what to the people of his day seemed impossible and unthinkable seems to us, in our day, inevitable.[12]

Wilberforce brought many gifts into this struggle. For one thing, he was gifted at working with a variety of people, including many with opposing political views on other subjects. Also, he was a gifted speaker; his close friend William Pitt, prime minister of England, said, "Of all the men I knew, Wilberforce has the greatest natural eloquence."[13]

Yet he always knew that he could not complete this assignment in his own power. It was just too big. In addition, he struggled with stress, depression, and digestive problems. He depended on God for strength and courage. "It is in thy power alone to deliver," he prayed. "I fly to thee for succour and support, O Lord let it come speedily, give me full proof of thy Almighty power; I am in great troubles, insurmountable by me, but to thee slight and inconsiderable . . . "[14]

It's a good thing Wilberforce remained faithful to God's call for his life, because it took twenty years to persuade Parliament to pass an act abolishing the slave trade. And then consider that this was just one of many reforms Wilberforce championed during his lifetime.

Today we look at the life of a man like Wilberforce with astonishment. And yet it's just one example of the weight God gives to what any of us can do when we are faithful to Him. We desperately need men and women who will faithfully live and lead God's way.

The power and authority to lead comes from God. His way is brokenness, uncommon communion, servanthood as an identity, and radical, immediate obedience. May these things characterize our lives and our leadership. May we bring the weight and the glory of God to bear on the work He has called us to do and to the world in which He has called us to do it.

"God, do it, I pray!"

NOTES

1. Nancy Leigh DeMoss, *Brokenness: The Heart God Revives* (Chicago: Moody, ©2002, 2005), 50.
2. Scott Rodin, "Becoming a Leader of No Reputation," *Journal of Religious Leadership* 1, no. 2 (fall 2002): 105–19.
3. "God delights in using ordinary people to accomplish extraordinary things," *Worldwide Challenge*, January 1976, 11.
4. Harold Myra and Marshall Shelley, *The Leadership Secrets of Billy Graham*, © 2005 Christianity Today International, (need info) page 127–28
5. Quotes taken from recollections posted on the website of the Eric Liddell Centre, ericliddell.org.
6. Barbara Hudson Powers, *The Henrietta Mears Story* (Grand Rapids: Fleming H. Revell, 1957), 114–15.
7. Powers, 125.
8. Ibid., 116.
9. Kevin Belmonte, *William Wilberforce: A Hero for Humanity* (Grand Rapids: Zondervan, 2007), 97.
10. Ibid., 91.
11. Eric Metaxas, "How William Wilberforce Changed the World," Wilberforce Forum, www.wilberforce.org.
12. Ibid.
13. Belefonte, 110.
14. Ibid., 108.

ISBN: 0-8024-8227-9
ISBN-13: 978-0-8024-8227-3

The biblical call to leadership must not be taken lightly.

J. Oswald Sanders presents and illustrates several magnifying principles through the lives of some prolific men—such as Moses, Nehemiah, Paul, David Livingstone, and Charles Spurgeon.

Spiritual Leadership will encourage you to place your talents and powers at God's disposal so you can become a leader used for His glory.

by J. Oswald Sanders
Find it now at your favorite local or online bookstore.
www.MoodyPublishers.com